Faculty Compensation Systems

Impact on the Quality of Higher Education

Terry P. Sutton, Peter J. Bergerson

ASHE-ERIC Higher Education Report Volume 28, Number 2
Adrianna J. Kezar, Series Editor

Prepared and published by

JOSSEY-BASS
A Wiley Company
San Francisco

In cooperation with

ERIC Clearinghouse on Higher Education
The George Washington University
URL: www.eriche.org

Association for the Study
of Higher Education
URL: www.tiger.coe.missouri.edu/~ashe

Graduate School of Education and Human Development
The George Washington University
URL: www.gwu.edu

Faculty Compensation Systems: Impact on the Quality of Higher Education
Terry P. Sutton, Peter J. Bergerson
ASHE-ERIC Higher Education Report Volume 28, Number 2
Adrianna J. Kezar, Series Editor

This publication was prepared partially with funding from the Office of Educational Research and Improvement, U.S. Department of Education, under contract no. ED-99-00-0036. The opinions expressed in this report do not necessarily reflect the positions or policies of OERI or the Department.

ISSN 0884-0040   ISBN 0-7879-5834-4

The ASHE-ERIC Higher Education Report is part of the Jossey-Bass Higher and Adult Education Series and is published six times a year by Jossey-Bass, 350 Sansome Street, San Francisco, California 94104-1342.

For subscription information, see the Back Issue/Subscription Order Form in the back of this journal.

Prospective authors are strongly encouraged to contact Adrianna Kezar, Director, ERIC Clearinghouse on Higher Education, at (202) 296-2597 ext. 14 or akezar@eric-he-edu.

Visit the Jossey-Bass Web site at **www.josseybass.com.**

Printed in the United States of America on acid-free recycled paper containing 100 percent recovered waste paper, of which at least 20 percent is postconsumer waste.

Executive Summary

Institutions of higher education face the challenge of reconciling external demands for public accountability with the internal demands for academic self-determination and faculty directed decision making. Active public intervention began in the 1980s because of "a torrent of criticism" (Bok, 1992, p. 14) emanating from a number of sources. A root cause of many of these criticisms was the application of profit-making principles to the management of higher education. Employing procedures used in the private sector such as cost benefit analysis and productivity studies to higher education institutions "leads to questions about increased waste . . . [and] less productive faculty members" (Winston, 1998, p. 18). In other words, the public debate changed from questions about education, learning, scholarship, and professional service to performance criteria measured in quantitative, business-like indicators, such as revenues earned and costs of operation. By 1998, more than half of the fifty states linked state appropriations of higher education funds to performance measures (Burke & Serban, 1998, p. 6).

What New Challenges Do Institutions Face in the Twenty-First Century?

Clearly, the rules have changed, and the new consumers have new concerns and challenges for higher education. In addition to controlling costs and promoting improvements in other business-like indicators, institutions of higher education are being required to answer questions about the quality of their service. The word *quality* has many different meanings, but the one used in this report defines institutional educational quality as the institution's meeting the goals set forth in its institutional mission (Green, 1994, p. 15).

A mission-driven measure of institutional quality implies that an institution should examine all means at its disposal to ensure that its mission is being supported by all members of the campus community, including faculty. Faculty compensation is one of the means an institution can use to achieve its mission. Moreover, faculty compensation is a management tool academic administrators can use to meet external demands for cost control, faculty performance, and institutional quality.

What Issues Address Faculty Compensation and Institutional Quality?

This report focuses on the following main points:

- The link between the particular faculty compensation system in place and its impact on institutional mission and quality.
- The various external and internal factors that affect the amount of compensation that faculty receive.
- How the absolute and relative levels of faculty compensation have changed over time and how general economic conditions and current events have affected faculty compensation.
- An examination of the different types of compensation systems used and how they operate. In general, faculty merit compensation and single salary systems are the most common types of systems in use, but several nontraditional systems have been reported in the literature.
- The intellectual rationale for the two primary types of faculty compensation systems in use.
- Operational advantages and disadvantages of the faculty compensation systems.
- How an institution can develop an effective faculty compensation system.
- What type of faculty compensation system can be recommended for different institutions.

Contents

Foreword

Faculty compensation mostly is not discussed. The silence is occasionally broken by the *Chronicle of Higher Education*'s annual report on faculty salaries or stories about disparities in pay between women and men. Administrative salaries, particularly those of presidents, make headlines, especially for the highest paid executives. But faculty salaries do not often spark heated debate.

This situation may change, however. Recent attacks on tenure, the rise in faculty and teaching assistant unionization, increased accountability, and other forces suggest that compensation systems may become central in discussions of higher education. First, the challenge to tenure has often been coupled with suggestions to increase or modify faculty compensation, making it more attractive to high quality individuals, even if a tenure system is not in place. Second, the revival of unionization and the growth of graduate student unionization will result in more debate about appropriate salary schemes, especially in an era of changing faculty roles and rising demands for accountability. Third, as colleges decide to experiment with new accountability schemes such as requiring faculty to be on campus a certain number of days and workload analysis, traditional faculty compensation systems may need to be reexamined. Traditional schemes have allowed faculty flexible schedules in exchange for lower salaries. Accountability suggests providing merit pay for those who perform well.

Within this context, a new ASHE-ERIC monograph by Terry Sutton and Peter Bergerson, *Faculty Compensation Systems: Impact on the Quality of Higher Education,* provides needed history, theory, and reconceptualization. The authors' diverse disciplinary backgrounds and their long-time participation in academe provide sharp insight. The monograph begins with an overview of the factors affecting compensation systems, providing a model for understanding this complex process. Next, the authors review the two major systems of compensation—a single salary schedule and merit pay. Most important, they present some alternative systems that have emerged and provide direction for the future. These alternative approaches are illustrated through case studies of innovative institutions that use them. This monograph deviates from other texts by examining the assumptions undergirding compensation systems that relate to motivations and impacts. One of the most problematic features of compensation systems is that the mismatch between means and ends and the reasons and goals for compensation systems is usually not examined. Therefore, the system often fails to bring about desired results. Based on an understanding of these assumptions and an institution's goals, an effective faculty compensation system can be developed. The concluding recommendations will help to reexamine the process on your campus. I invite you to review these important ideas, which will be critical in the next decade.

Several other ASHE-ERIC monographs examine related issues. *Budgeting for Higher Education at the State Level* is an important complement that will help policymakers make more effective decisions, and *Managing Costs in Higher Education* reviews compensation issues in relation to other campus expenses. I hope these resources help to make the complex decisions related to faculty compensation that lie ahead.

Adrianna Kezar
Series Editor,
ASHE-ERIC Higher Education Report Series
Assistant Professor,
The George Washington University

Acknowledgments

The authors are particularly grateful to Adrianna Kezar, series editor and director of the ERIC Clearinghouse on Higher Education, for her encouragement, assistance, and patience. We are most grateful to Charles Kupchella, president of the University of North Dakota–Grand Forks and former provost at Southeast Missouri State University, for his academic interest and financial commitment to this work. At Southeast, we also wish to thank Gerald McDougall, dean of the Donald L. Harrison College of Business; and the faculty of the Department of Economics, particularly Bruce Domazlicky, for their sage advice, encouragement, and willingness to debate the topics examined. We recognize and appreciate the research collection work of Theresa Haug, graduate assistant in the Department of Political Science, and the computer expertise of Marie Steinhoff, secretary for the Department of Marketing.

To those who anonymously reviewed our manuscript: we appreciate your careful reading and thoughtful comments. This work has been enhanced by your suggestions.

This work is dedicated to our wives, Sharon Sutton and Connie Bergerson, whose words of wisdom, guidance, advice, encouragement, and support were a welcome source of inspiration.

Introduction

INSTITUTIONS OF HIGHER EDUCATION in the United States face a variety of issues, including demands for more accountability, concerns about the quality of higher education, and increasing external intervention in academic decision making. A number of educators (see, for example, Bok, 1992; Lenington, 1996; Winston, 1998) have published essays outlining the various issues facing higher education at the time of writing. But one issue, the productivity of higher education institutions in light of rising tuition and fees, has became a primary public concern that in turn has led to criticisms of how faculty spend their time and set the stage for a "debate about faculty roles" (McMahon & Caret, 1997, p. 11) and how institutional monies are used to reward faculty activity. In the last few years, higher education began to be judged in terms of profit-making principles applicable to private businesses, which "leads to questions about increased waste . . . [and] less productive faculty members" (Winston, 1998, p. 18). This transformation from an academic model for governing higher education to a business model and its accompanying profit-making principles has taken place in California and New York. The California State University (CSU) system hired "one of a new breed of 'corporate chancellors,' showing a business sense and an enthusiasm for accountability that have gained him great support among trustees and California lawmakers" (Selingo, 1999, p. A32). Dr. Charles B. Reed, the new chancellor at CSU, aggressively plans to increase the quality of higher education in the system by using "merit pay, along with Cornerstones [Cal State's strategic plan] and other plans, to increase Cal State's visibility in the

Legislature . . . and to show lawmakers that he's holding the system's professors and students accountable" (Selingo, 1999, p. A33).

A similar situation exists at the City University of New York (CUNY). A political debate broke out over the future direction of the system that has produced a "tumultuous period of reform" (Healy & Hebel, 1999, p. A34). The governor of New York appointed a new chair of the CUNY board of trustees, whose primary goal is to improve the quality of the CUNY system by, among other things, increased accountability for academic programs (p. A34). The California and New York examples can be viewed as harbingers of issues and concerns that every institution of higher education will likely encounter in the near future.

In an attempt to control the cost of public higher education, "almost half the state governments are turning toward direct intervention in the inner working of the academy" (American Association of University Professors, 1996, p. 46). In the early 1990s, elected officials began to abandon a basically laissez-faire attitude toward higher education; for example, "in January, 1991, the Maryland State Legislature began actively examining the workloads of college faculty" (McMahon & Caret, 1997, p. 12).

The Maryland legislature was eventually convinced that faculty are engaged in a long work week but remained "unconvinced that faculty are using their time productively" (American Association of University Professors, 1996, p. 49). Further, some states began to reward institutions that succeeded in achieving specific goals. In Missouri, for example, a Funding for Results program granted public universities additional funding for achieving certain legislative goals, including graduating minority students, improving student retention, and graduating students in "critical high-skill trades and disciplines" (Missouri Coordinating Board for Higher Education, 1998, pp. 45–46). In 1996, the South Carolina legislature instituted "performance funding that linked a portion of the state's support for public colleges to their success in meeting certain quantifiable standards." . . . and puts no more than 5 percent of any institution's budget at stake (Schmidt, 1999, p. A26). A noteworthy feature of the South Carolina plan is how it provides "institutions financial incentives to increase faculty workload" (p. A28). In South Carolina, the quantitative measures on which institutions are judged include the relative comparative position of average institutional faculty compensation to national averages (p. A26).

The South Carolina experience suggests that higher education institutions have come under increasing external scrutiny and are being forced to reconsider and justify administrative policies that were not public policy concerns in the past. These policy concerns include the quality of the institution and its faculty compensation. Faculty compensation has become "a rather prominent element in the recent attention paid to college and university productivity [and among] . . . central administrators aiming to manage rising costs [because] . . . they are unquestionably central to the productivity of the enterprise" (Hearn, 1999, p. 391).

Throughout the variety of criticisms of higher education, faculty compensation represents the single common element. As institutional policymakers develop an agenda for the new decade, faculty compensation must be considered an important factor in achieving an institution's goals. Institutions need to ask themselves what kind of institution they want to be and how they can achieve those goals. For an institution that wishes to increase its faculty productivity, become cost efficient, and achieve an improved public perception, faculty compensation represents an important additional management tool that can be used.

> **As institutional policymakers develop an agenda for the new decade, faculty compensation must be considered an important factor in achieving an institution's goals.**

To maintain high quality higher education in the United States, its institutions need to examine carefully how faculty compensation is determined and understand how different compensation systems influence faculty activity. Unfortunately, "surprisingly little effort has been made to assemble the most basic facts about the characteristics of faculty salary systems" (Hansen, 1988, p. 10). Moreover, "too much of the recent attention to the topic [of pay and performance in higher education] has been based on anecdotal and incomplete information" (Hearn, 1999, p. 392).

The audiences this report addresses are those concerned with faculty compensation and the impact compensation systems have on the quality of higher education and the higher education community: faculty members, university administrators, members of governing boards, governors, state legislators, and financial contributors.

This report addresses nine subthemes:

1. What constitutes higher education institutional quality, and how is faculty compensation related to institutional quality?
2. What affects the level of funding supporting institutional faculty compensation, and what is the relationship of faculty compensation, institutional mission, and public perceptions about institutional effectiveness?
3. How has actual and real faculty compensation varied over time?
4. How are the different faculty compensation systems actually used to determine faculty compensation, and how do these systems operate?
5. What are the theoretical and philosophical foundations of each type of faculty compensation system?
6. What are the operational advantages and disadvantages of each type of faculty compensation system?
7. What goals and objectives should a compensation system address?
8. How can an institution construct an effective faculty compensation system?
9. What constitutes the most appropriate faculty compensation system for faculty at an institution?

The next section discusses the first of these subthemes.

Institutional Quality and Faculty Compensation

INSTITUTIONAL QUALITY is a value-laden term and can be defined in a variety of ways. A workable definition places a premium on achieving the institution's mission. Therefore, "a high quality institution is one that clearly states its mission (or purpose) and is efficient and effective in meeting the goals that it has set itself" (Green, 1994, p. 15). Thus, the quality of an institution depends on the degree to which the institution has succeeded in fulfilling its mission.

Adopting achievement of institutional mission as a measure of quality in higher education means that the achievement of quality becomes an ongoing, continuous process, with quality being accomplished by making the institution's policies, processes, and procedures (including the faculty compensation system) consistent with its mission. Because institutions of higher education rely so heavily on the behavior and actions of the faculty, it becomes vital for an institution to realize that "because how we reward faculty largely determines what faculty do, the time has come for all governing boards to examine the promotion and tenure system in light of their institution's mission" (Diamond, 1993b, p. 17).

The impact of faculty compensation on the quality of higher education forms the underlying issue addressed in this report. Moreover, two subpremises together form the report's overall conceptual premise. These stem from common sense, casual observation, and numerous scholarly sources found in the literature on higher education faculty compensation (Benjamin, 1998; Marchant and Newman, 1994; Lillydahl and Singell, 1993;

Miller, 1992; Taylor, Hunnicutt, and Keeffe, 1991). They lead to the following conclusions:

1. The absolute and relative levels of faculty compensation have an impact on faculty behavior.
2. Faculty behavior and its relationship to the employing institution's mission can be positive, negative, or neutral, depending on the specific details of the compensation system in use.

A variety of factors influence an institution's quality, with faculty compensation one that is often overlooked. An institution wishing to restructure in an effort to change its quality should keep in mind that "no fundamental restructuring [of an institution] can occur until the current incentive system governing faculty behavior is changed" (Benjamin, 1998, p. 16).

The literature reveals that faculty compensation and its impact on the mission and quality of higher education have not been examined systematically, "so little evidence is available to help understand the implications of one [compensation] system versus another" (Hansen, 1988, p. 13). What is available are numerous scholarly journal articles that examine small parts of the general topic. This report analyzes, orders, and presents the findings of research on faculty compensation in a cogent summary form; it includes a list of references providing in-depth sources for readers seeking more information.

Factors Affecting Faculty Compensation

Institutions have limited control over the amount of funding available to finance faculty compensation. For example, decisions that determine the amount of funds available for faculty compensation often come from external or environmental forces that the institution cannot fully control. The variety of forces that affect the amount of funding for higher education faculty compensation suggest an ongoing, continual cycle creating a loop. Figure 1 presents a hypothetical feedback model addressing the wide range of factors that educators need to keep in mind when attempting to change faculty compensation.

Figure 1 implies that each institution needs to scan its environment continuously to be aware of public perception and the attitudes of political actors

FIGURE 1
Institutional Funding Feedback Mechanism

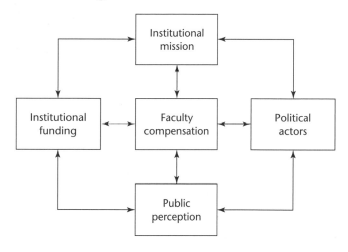

and thus be able to respond effectively to the demands of these groups. The modern higher education environment forces each institution to be cognizant of its role as an economic, social, and cultural agent for the stakeholders it serves. The model presented in Figure 1 includes the following characteristics:

1. The public's perception of how well an institution is fulfilling its mission affects the amount of institutional funding the public will support (Foldesi, 1996, p. 30; Breslin and Klagholz, 1980, p. 44).
2. The level of funding an institution acquires directly affects the level of faculty compensation.
3. The level and structure of the faculty compensation system affect the institution's success in fulfilling its mission.

Internal Factors Determining Faculty Compensation

Internal to the institution are specific factors that determine faculty compensation, the various faculty attributes, and activities that are rewarded within the institution. They include academic rank, faculty productivity, market pay in the discipline, ability to obtain external grants, seniority or length of service to the institution, service in administrative positions, professional service, graduate teaching and guidance, and other factors such as gender, race, and age. At some institutions, differences in compensation may result from purely subjective factors, for example, "physical proximity to the chairman's office" (Hooker, 1978, p. 48).

Empirical studies of factors that affect individual faculty compensation typically have found that "generally the best predictor of salary within an institution and within any rank are an individual's years of experience" (Lewis, 1996, p. 46). An increasing number of articles published is second (Tuckman and Tuckman, 1976, p. 55). Publication of scholarly journal articles enables individual faculty members to be promoted more rapidly, and once the top rank is reached, publication enables an individual's compensation to continue to rise. Publishing a book is not as rewarding as publishing an article; it appears that "the marginal returns to research effort appear to be fairly low, even if the salary increments attributable to publication are projected over the faculty member's lifetime . . . [and] the returns to book publication may be less than the returns to article publication" (Tuckman and Tuckman, 1976, p. 62). Evidence that research and publication significantly affect a faculty member's compensation level appears in other studies (see, for example, Fairweather, 1993a, p. 64, 1995, p. 189; Hunnicutt, Taylor, and Keeffe, 1991, p. 19; Kasten, 1984, pp. 512–513; Marchant and Newman, 1994, p. 150; Prewitt, Phillips, and Yasin, 1991, p. 413).

These studies seem to suggest that faculty rewards for teaching are minimal at best. "Research on the relationship between teaching and rewards has been inconclusive" (Kasten, 1984, p. 501). Kasten cites eleven studies since 1970 that reached different conclusions about teaching and faculty rewards.

Working in an administrative position on campus directly increases an individual faculty member's compensation three ways. First, because of the extra responsibilities, compensation increases. Second, administrative positions are typically eleven- or twelve-month positions, while teaching and research positions are typically for nine months. Third, "those with a previous history of administrative activity also receive high salaries, primarily because the increases they receive while acting in an administrative role are not taken away when they return to a research or teaching position" (Tuckman and Tuckman, 1976, pp. 59–60).

Characteristics of an Ideal Faculty Compensation System

The hypothetical faculty compensation funding feedback model in Figure 1 provides the foundation for determining characteristics of an ideal faculty compensation system:

1. "The value, vision, mission, and goals of the organization must be clearly and specifically defined so all the participants know what the end objectives are" (Chaffee and Sherr, 1992, p. xix). In other words, there exists within the institution "shared values and unity of purpose [along with] constancy of purpose (Cornesky, McCool, Byrnes, and Weber, 1992, p. 9).
2. "Each individual, in some way, must accept personal responsibility for achieving the goals and accomplishing the mission of the organization" (Chaffee and Sherr, 1992, p. xx). Institutional quality will be enhanced because of an "emphasis on responsibility to contribute (Cornesky, McCool, Byrnes, and Weber, 1992, p. 9).
3. Faculty performing satisfactorily must receive a constant standard of living, while faculty performing at an above satisfactory level should receive appropriately increased compensation.
4. Faculty must believe the compensation system is administered objectively and without any subjective bias.

These characteristics of the ideal compensation model should be kept in mind as benchmarks against which the characteristics of actual or suggested compensation systems in the following pages can be compared. In sum, the model faculty compensation system "must be compatible with the institution's central mission. [Further,] the institutional reward system must send a clear signal to faculty that what is valued by the institution will be rewarded at all points in the promotion and tenure system" (Diamond, 1993b, p. 6).

Faculty Compensation: A Historical Perspective

BEFORE EXAMINING different faculty compensation systems, it will be helpful to review a brief history of faculty compensation to provide background and a foundation for the rest of the report. Data on higher education faculty compensation during the twentieth century reveal eight time periods when real faculty compensation increased and six time periods when it declined (Bowen, 1978, p. 5; Bell, 2000, p. 14). A publication helpful in understanding the pattern that has been evident during this period is *Academic Compensation: Are Faculty and Staff in American Higher Education Adequately Paid?* (Bowen, 1978). Bowen's data include information from the 1903–04 to 1976–77 academic years (p. 5). Table 1 shows how annual real faculty compensation (RFC) (actual or nominal compensation adjusted for price changes) varied with different general economic conditions.

An analysis of faculty compensation during the twentieth century reveals that during three periods with steady national economic growth and stable prices (an inflation rate less than 3.5 percent annually), faculty in higher education realized moderate increases in real compensation. Conversely, real faculty compensation fell during periods of moderate to high rates of inflation in three periods. The period from 1981 to 2000 was one of moderate increases in real faculty compensation.

One can infer from Table 1 that faculty in higher education benefit economically along with other members of society during periods of economic growth and moderate inflation but at a lower relative increment than professions in other fields. Moreover, because the rate of real growth in faculty compensation has historically been moderate, the rate of compensation increases

---

TABLE 1

Annual Percentage Changes in Real Faculty Compensation and the Consumer Price Index

Period	National Economic Condition	Annual CPI Change	Annual RFC Change
1903–04 to 1913–14	Steady growth, stable prices	+1.0%	+1.1%
1913–14 to 1919–20	Rapid growth, high inflation	+11.0	−5.3
1919–20 to 1922–23	Recession, deflation	−3.2	+10.7
1922–23 to 1929–30	Steady growth, stable prices	0.0	+1.4
1929–30 to 1931–32	Severe recession, deflation	−7.6	+8.9
1931–32 to 1934–35	Depression, deflation	−2.1	−2.9
1934–35 to 1939–40	Recovery, stable prices	+0.6	+1.5
1939–40 to 1942–43	Growing recovery, moderate inflation	+6.4	−4.9
1942–43 to 1945–46	Prosperity, inflation	+3.8	+2.9
1945–46 to 1951–52	Uneven economic growth, inflation	+5.8	−0.9
1951–52 to 1969–70	Steady growth, growing inflation	+2.0	+3.6
1969–70 to 1976–77	Uneven growth, high inflation	+6.5	−0.3
1976–77 to 1979–80	Steady growth, high inflation	+19.3	−4.4
1981–82 to 1997–98	Steady growth, stable prices	+3.4	+1.1

Note: Results from 1903–04 to 1976–77 are from Bowen, 1978, p. 5, those from 1976–77 to 1997–98 from Bell, 1998, p. 16. Bowen divided the period 1903 to 1977 into twelve periods of varying length according to consistent general economic conditions; data have been added from 1978 to 2000 as reported by Bell (2000, pp. 13–22). The descriptions of economic conditions in this table are taken from Bowen's work except for the period from academic year 1976–77 to academic year 1999–00, which were taken from Bell (2000, p. 13).
Sources: Bowen, 1978, p. 5; Bell, 1998, p. 16.

does not hamper faculty morale in general. (See Lillydahl and Singell, 1993, for verification of this conclusion.)

As these data indicate, there have been varying degrees of support for faculty compensation in the twentieth century. "Something changed around the beginning of World War II" (Bowen, 1978, p. 6). During periods of general economic stability and growth, real faculty compensation increased overall at four times the rate it had before the war. Moreover, inflation in the period from 1945 to 1952 did not result in decreases in real faculty compensation.

This favorable period toward higher education in general was attributed to "a new appreciation of higher education as a source of economic productivity and national power" (Bowen, 1968, p. 17). Several cultural phenomena, ranging from the results of World War II and advances in atomic energy, the launching of *Sputnik* by Russia, the U.S. space program, and a general desire of parents to provide a better future for their children, all contributed to this change in public attitude toward higher education (p. 17).

The last quarter of the twentieth century produced several additional developments. "Since 1977, . . . several important developments have influenced faculty salaries. Market pressures and competition for faculties have resulted in compression, and in some fields, inversion, of traditional salary structures" (Lillydahl and Singell, 1993, p. 234). Salary compression occurs when new faculty obtain relatively higher starting salaries than those received by experienced faculty. Inversion occurs when new faculty start at salaries higher than their more experienced colleagues. If compression and inversion occur at an institution, it becomes highly probable that the more experienced faculty would become dissatisfied with their own compensation and with the institution.

Besides changes in real faculty compensation, another issue of interest in higher education is how real faculty compensation compares to that earned by equally well-educated workers outside higher education. This factor is of concern because of the factors that would be present if real faculty compensation were significantly lower than in alternative employment opportunities:

1. Some high-quality faculty will leave academia for employment external to higher education.
2. Faculty in disciplines with relatively high external real compensation will be granted "market pay" that is higher than the compensation received by faculty in other disciplines to keep them in higher education. Faculty in disciplines such as medicine, engineering, and business typically are hired at compensation levels higher than colleagues in other disciplines.
3. High-quality individuals will not have an incentive to pursue a career in academia if faculty compensation in higher education is low relative to occupations outside higher education.

Bowen's study outlines the relative changes between real faculty compensation and workers employed outside higher education for the period 1904 to

1977. Academics have experienced a smaller annual percentage change in actual (unadjusted for inflation) compensation than all civilian full-time employees. When compared with external professional employment, professors currently earn 42 percent less (Bell, 1998, p. 15). For example, a professor of foreign languages who specializes in Spanish earns less than he or she could earn as an employee of a business firm that buys or sells products with firms in Spanish-speaking nations. This comparison was performed for external professional workers with at least eighteen years of education. On the other hand, faculty compensation is more stable compared with other professional workers. For example, professional workers outside higher education experienced a significant decrease in compensation from 1986 through 1988, while faculty compensation continued to rise slowly (Bell, 1998, p. 17) which could be the result of factors unique to that period. The national economy was not in a recession in that period because real gross domestic product grew at an annual rate of more than 2.5 percent (*Economic Report of the President*, 1997, p. 303). Another difference is that there is less variance among faculty salaries from the highest to the lowest than there is among the salaries of external professionals.

Academics have experienced a smaller annual percentage change in actual (unadjusted for inflation) compensation than all civilian full-time employees.

Even though faculty earn less than comparable professionals, this deficiency is offset by some financial and working environment advantages. The advantages include "fringe benefits, outside sources of income, opportunities for subsidized travel, extended holidays and leaves, relatively low costs of living in smaller communities. . . . [Further, there are] intangible rewards such as employment security, control over one's work, participation in the cultural life of the college or university, [a] sense of performing work of high social value. . . ." (Bowen, 1968, p. 12). The standing of higher education faculty compensation relative to that of other professionals is a topic that should be examined in more detail than is currently available for the recent past.

This review sets the stage for the topics that follow. The next section discusses the different types of faculty compensation systems in use in higher education.

Faculty Compensation Systems Used in Higher Education

HIGHER EDUCATION INSTITUTIONS in the United States compensate faculty with one of three types of systems:

1. "The contract salary system . . . , wherein each faculty member negotiates his or her annual salary with the employing institution" (Beaumont, 1985, p. 3). A contract salary system is often referred to as merit pay.
2. "The single salary schedule . . . based on an officially specified salary for each academic rank. It includes a fixed schedule of salary steps within each rank and a normal, time-in-step specification for each salary step" (Beaumont, 1985, p. 3).
3. A nontraditional faculty compensation system, which includes any compensation system other than a pure single salary schedule or merit system.

The faculty compensation literature disagrees about which of the first two types of faculty compensation systems is more common. Beaumont (1985, p. 3) says "the predominant system in the United States is the contract salary system," while Keane (1978, p. 6), from a study performed during the same time period as Beaumont's, reports that of eighty-two small private colleges, twenty-eight had ongoing faculty merit plans. In 1988, Hansen reported that "the prevalence of these two different salary systems [contract salary system and single salary schedule] and their various combinations cannot be established because so little information exists on the allocation of annual salary increases at different colleges and universities" (p. 11). A reasonable conclusion is that nontraditional faculty compensation systems are the least common.

The uncertainty about what type of faculty compensation system is the most common is a question that deserves further investigation by scholars.

Contract Salary System or Merit Pay

A contract salary system or merit compensation system uses institutionally specified criteria that reflect the expected productivity of a newly hired faculty member to establish that faculty member's initial compensation level. Typically, an institution with a faculty merit compensation system uses measures of faculty productivity such as the level of educational preparation, length of experience, and amount of scholarly activity. Teaching effectiveness can also be used to measure productivity if those involved can agree about its definition. Service activity can also be used if the institution considers professional service important. An example of a merit evaluation form is provided in Appendix A. This form, a detailed itemization of various faculty activities used to determine a faculty member's productivity, was used to evaluate Department of Nursing professors at Ball State University in 1986 (Elliott and Ryan, 1986, p. 132). Other disciplines may not include the same specific items, but the form provides a good schematic to follow in developing a list of criteria. Some weight variation is implicit in the form in Appendix A. For instance, under "teaching," seven criteria are mandatory, while a faculty member must meet at least two of the other six. Other departments can vary the weighting to agree with their own valuations of relative importance.

Single Salary Schedule

A single salary schedule assigns each newly hired faculty member to a step or cell in a matrix based on education and experience to determine that faculty member's initial compensation. Every faculty member receives an equal percentage increase, a fixed dollar increase, or some combination of percentage and fixed dollar increase whenever the compensation level is increased, usually annually. A single salary schedule is generally administered by developing a grid or matrix with academic rank as one criterion and years of experience as the other. An example of a single salary schedule is shown in Table 2.

TABLE 2
Example of a Single Salary Schedule

	Steps				
Rank	1	2	3	4	5
Professor II	65,389	68,716	72,092	75,667	79,622
Professor I	62,211	65,389	68,716	72,092	75,667
Associate Professor II	51,239	53,821	56,452	59,282	62,253
Associate Professor I	48,856	51,239	53,821	56,452	61,765
Assistant Professor II	40,564	42,550	44,685	46,919	49,253
Assistant Professor I	38,578	40,564	42,550	44,685	46,919
Instructor II	36,791	38,578	40,564	42,550	44,685
Instructor I	35,003	36,791	38,578	40,564	42,550

Source: Beaumont, 1978, p. 20, adjusted for changes in the consumer price index from 1971 to 2000.

To construct a single salary schedule, an institution must determine the minimal level of academic training and experience that a potential faculty member must possess to be offered continuing faculty appointment. Second, the institution must decide the different dollar amounts in each cell, both horizontally and vertically. The dollar level of compensation associated with a cell can be any value the institution deems appropriate.

Nontraditional Faculty Compensation Systems

A few institutions use nontraditional compensation systems and have published reports on them. This section discusses these alternative or nontraditional compensation systems.

Faculty Self-Development Review

This suggestion involves a self-development review based on employees' needs, growth, and satisfaction to integrate their achievement with organizational goals (Tharp, 1991, pp. 75–76). Increased faculty productivity results from changing faculty evaluations to emphasize growth and self-development and changing the compensation system to make it "rooted in the traditions and organizational climate of the institution" (pp. 77–78). Implicitly, this compensation system assumes that such a compensation system will give faculty members incentive to improve themselves in a way aligned with the mission of the institution. Under Tharp's suggestion, the individual institution would establish its own details for a faculty self-development review system.

An actual compensation system that represents a similar system occurred when Georgia State University adopted a posttenure review system in 1983. The element similar to Tharp's self-development review is the posttenure review of faculty. Georgia State conducted posttenure review of faculty through peer and administrative review.

> *The process begins with the chair's assessment of the faculty member's effectiveness in teaching, research or creative activity, and service. [After progressing through the institution's sequence of review by faculty peer groups and supervisors] . . . the faculty member receives copies of all the reports and discusses them at a joint conference with the chair, the dean, and the area associate dean.*
>
> *The purpose of the conference is to identify the most constructive ways of developing and advancing the faculty member's academic objectives and, ideally, arriving at a 5-year plan for achieving these objectives. This requires listening carefully to the faculty member's ideas and entering into a creative discussion of the options for achieving optimal productivity. While the various reports provide the framework for discussion, the faculty member's input is essential. (Abdelal, Blumenfeld, Crimmins, and Dressel, 1997, p. 66)*

Georgia State reports a higher level of faculty productivity and higher faculty morale using this system (Abdelal, Blumenfeld, Crimmins, and Dressel, 1997, pp. 68, 71), but the institution continues to cope with establishing objective criteria for judgments (pp. 69–70).

Single Salary Component Combined with Merit Increases

Combination compensation systems with a single salary component to adjust for annual cost of living increases reserved for faculty evaluated to be performing at a satisfactory level, plus a merit component to be awarded to faculty evaluated to be producing at an above satisfactory level can be found at a variety of institutions (Elliott and Ryan, 1986; MacKay, 1985; Manaster, 1985), including the authors' home institution. A combination system has features that have been cited as perhaps "ideal" (Eymonerie, 1980, p. 119).

Ball State Combination System. Ball State University implemented its combination system in the early 1980s. Faculty activity considered to represent higher level productivity was defined as anything that makes a faculty member more marketable in higher education. Implementation involved two steps: (1) colleges' and departments' establishment of their own guidelines for increases in compensation in excess of the cost of living adjustment, and (2) "a system for distributing the money [developed] at the department level" (Elliott and Ryan, 1986, p. 130).

Appendix B presents the evaluative form for satisfactory faculty productivity in the Nursing Department at Ball State (Elliott and Ryan, 1986, p. 130). Like the merit components listed in Appendix A (also from Ball State), the elements presented in Appendix B may not be applicable to all disciplines.

Oakland University Combination System. Oakland University in Rochester, Michigan, instituted another version of a combined single salary schedule and contract salary compensation system in 1970 (McKay, 1985, pp. 17–22). Faculty members are placed on the single salary structure at a certain level, earning a minimum dollar salary at that level. Differences from one salary level minimum to the next "[translate] into about a 3 percent increase in salary, with larger increases for junior level faculty and smaller or no increases for senior associate professors and senior full professors" (p. 21). When a year passes, a faculty member's placement increases by one level. "Promotion usually involves an additional level advancement and there are occasional special level advancements" (p. 19).

Merit increases at Oakland University are referred to as the "personal factor" (McKay, 1985, p. 19), which have minimum and maximum values to be multiplied by the faculty member's salary minimum to find the total salary. The personal factor an individual faculty member receives "should correspond to collegial judgment of the person's individual professional merit . . . [by] the individual academic unit" (p. 21).

McKay reported in 1985 that the system had been in place since 1970–71, which he views as an indication that the faculty at Oakland University are satisfied with it (p. 22).

California Combination System. The University of California implemented a combined single salary schedule and merit system in the 1970s (Manaster, 1985). This approach, referred to as the "step system," uses a salary scale with fourteen steps (four for assistant professors, three for associate professors, and seven for full professors) that is usually revised every year. The University of California also established "a special salary scale for faculty in business/ management and engineering" (p. 25) that ranged from 9.6 to 33.3 percent higher than for other faculty.

Once the scale has been determined, the step system is implemented by placing a faculty member in the appropriate spot on the scale. In subsequent years, any higher compensation level for a single faculty member is obtained by adjusting the scale for cost of living or promoting him or her to a higher step based on merit. To reach the highest step, a faculty member must demonstrate "evidence of great scholarly distinction and national recognition, highly meritorious service, and evidence of excellent university teaching. . . . Finally, it is possible for faculty to advance to an above-scale salary, but such advancement is reserved for scholars and teachers of the highest distinction, whose work has been internationally recognized and acclaimed" (Manaster, 1985, p. 24). Promotion in the California step system is initiated by a department chair after conferring with faculty colleagues. After that, the recommendation for promotion is sent through a standing committee of the Academic Senate, then to a secret ad hoc committee, and finally to the administration (p. 25). This system "has worked well . . . [with] reasonable expectations and fairly uniform treatment of the faculty. It also appears to contain adequate flexibility to reward outstanding accomplishment and to provide members of the faculty with incentives throughout their careers. . . . On the other hand, the system of making academic personnel decisions is often viewed as cumbersome . . . and may need to be streamlined" (p. 26).

Community College Combination System. A combination single salary and merit compensation system used at Williamsport Area Community College employs a "two-dimensional [matrix] with the vertical steps representing teaching and trade experience and the horizontal steps representing educational preparation" (Bowers and Breuder, 1982, p. 33). The values in the matrix attempt to define "salary equivalence . . . for a faculty with diverse preparation and experience" (pp. 33–34). Faculty at the college have incentive to improve their educational preparation and move horizontally across the matrix instead of just accumulating year after year of experience and moving only vertically down the matrix. It generally takes two years of experience to move to a higher "unit value . . . which in turn is translated into an appropriate dollar amount to be added to a predetermined base salary" (p. 33). Consequently, if a long-term faculty member gives up trying to improve and become more productive, that faculty member's compensation increases at a slower rate than that of a less senior, more productive faculty member.

This method could be altered to make the vertical steps represent levels of increased faculty productivity for comprehensive four-year institutions. Changes in the cost of living could be accounted for by increasing the level of compensation in each cell of the matrix by a percentage equal to the cost of living change.

Contract Merit System with Voluntary Participation

This system, established by the Department of Education at Eastern Washington University (Shreeve and others, 1985, p. 155), requires each faculty member who wants to receive a merit increase to develop a plan before the academic year begins specifying the level of merit that he or she will work toward and specifying the way this level will be reached. The EWU merit system requires each faculty member to decide independently whether or not to apply for a merit increase. With an affirmative decision, the faculty member then has to decide what level of merit to work toward. The next step requires a development plan generated by the faculty member to be submitted to the department's merit pay committee. At the end of the academic period covered by the plan, the faculty member submits a report to that committee for review and verification. If the faculty member has been successful in meeting the plan, that faculty member receives merit pay.

Under a contract merit system, faculty decide what type and what amount of activity will be included in their development plans and how to document this activity. All faculty accomplishing their individualized plans receive a merit reward. A contract merit compensation system could be combined with a single salary system to provide faculty who are producing at a satisfactory level a compensation increment equal to cost of living increases.

Salary Administration with a Merit Compensation System

The term "salary administration" means that institutions take an active role in managing faculty and staff compensation to control costs, avoid discriminatory and subjective decision making on faculty salaries, and promote other goals of the institution (Van Fleet, 1972, pp. 413–414). All institutionally valued faculty activities are assigned point values or weights that can range from zero to a finite or infinite upper limit. Each faculty member's points are determined by evaluation, and merit compensation adjustments are assigned on the basis of relative cumulative points when compared with those of all other faculty.

The establishment of a salary administration faculty compensation system involves following three steps: (1) form a salary committee of faculty, administrators, and a student, which (2) constructs a scale, along with weights for meritorious faculty activity, and (3) tests the scale and revises it if necessary (Van Fleet, 1972, p. 414).

Once the size of the budget to support compensation increases is determined, an institution using this procedure must determine how to allocate the available funds to faculty. Either the salary committee or a faculty governance group could make the decision.

Adjusting Relative Faculty Compensation for Unjustified Distortions. With any type of annual merit faculty compensation system, relative faculty compensation may be distorted and not accurately reflect the relative levels of performance by the faculty. These distortions may occur because of "fluctuations in funding levels from year to year" (Clevenger, 1989, p. 8) or differences in subjective evaluation of different faculty within a department, between departments, or between colleges. To correct for these distortions, institutions can use an approach called a "salary model" (p. 8). A salary model can be constructed by any institution as a means to check for the presence of compensation distortions or inequities by using computer software such as regression analysis. Such a review of relative faculty compensation may be conducted annually or every few years to oversee the appropriateness of an institution's merit faculty compensation system. If application of the salary model reveals distortions, the model can be adjusted and corrected at any time.

Rewarding Teams of Faculty. The faculty compensation systems examined thus far, including the single salary schedule, base faculty compensation on the activities of an individual faculty member. But "the primary activities of most institutions of higher education (instruction, research, and service) are often jointly produced by faculty" (Layzell, 1996, p. 270). In other words, much of the productivity of faculty is the output of teams of faculty. To correct for this distortion in the way faculty rewards are determined, "why not aggregate the data [of a department's teaching, scholarship, and service] and then reward the most effective departments or divisions?" (Chait, 1988, p. 23). A small number of institutions of higher education have begun to reward departmental teamwork (see Wergin and Swingen, 1999).

Rewarding Professional Public Service. It has long been conventional wisdom in higher education that faculty fulfill three roles: teaching, research, and public service. Because of its long history as one of the three primary duties of higher education faculty, "public service should be but is not well rewarded in most university environments, and this absence of reward prevents the full development of outreach programs" (Florestano and Hambrick, 1984, p. 18). The type of faculty public service that should be rewarded is "'profession-related public service,' not the broader set of activities often included under 'public service'" (p. 18).

Requiring Faculty to Generate Compensation Funds. Some medical schools with clinics open to pay-for-paying patients have altered the way faculty salaries are determined for clinical professors. Medical faculty tend to earn some of the largest compensation paid to faculty in the nation. In the past, large revenues from teaching hospital clinics financed part of medical faculty compensation. With the rise of managed care, however, many clinics have received lower revenues from patients. The University of Texas medical school in Galveston "has adopted a compensation plan that divides a professor's salary into 'core' and 'at risk' portions. The guaranteed portion is set at 80 percent of the average salary reported by the American Association of Medical Colleges for professors in comparable jobs around the country. The rest fluctuates depending on how much money is brought in by professors and their departments" (Mangan, 1996, p. A16). This approach has been extended to research faculty who do not treat clinical patients by linking faculty compensation to external grant funds brought into the institution, similar to research institutions that have used external grants acquired as a measure of faculty productivity. Linking faculty compensation directly to funds brought in by an individual faculty member may in the future become more widespread if competition for institutional funding increases.

Linking faculty compensation directly to funds brought in by an individual faculty member may in the future become more widespread if competition for institutional funding increases.

Intellectual Rationale for Different Faculty Compensation Systems

INSTITUTIONS using one of the three types of faculty compensation systems discussed in the previous section have adopted their chosen system for a particular reason or reasons, which may be explicitly stated, implicitly understood, or simply to follow another institution's example. Whatever the faculty compensation system in use at an institution, faculty and administration should periodically review it to determine whether its rationale is consistent with the institution's goals.

For an institution that has reviewed its current faculty compensation system and determined a change is in order, some way to judge the optimal alternative system is needed. In other words, a conceptual lens is needed to interpret the impact of a particular faculty compensation system on faculty behavior. This section reviews the various intellectual arguments published in faculty compensation literature to support different systems. Such a discussion should aid in understanding why a particular compensation system may or may not be appropriate for a particular institution at a particular time.

The following discussion outlines the philosophical and theoretical arguments in support of merit faculty compensation and a single salary schedule for faculty. Adopting an alternative faculty compensation system is usually determined to be in the institution's best interests after it has lived with either a pure merit system or a pure single salary schedule for some time and decided that operational problems necessitate trying something else.

Arguments Supporting a Faculty Merit Compensation System

The intellectual roots supporting this form of compensation have been linked to the Protestant Reformation, where an individual's success is measured by the amount of extra output produced rather than by status or ancestral lineage (Evans, 1970, p. 726). In American culture, "the concept of merit pay encompasses the work values of the Puritan work ethic and the notion of Jeffersonian democracy that individual accomplishment should be based on ability rather than status" (Mickler, 1987, p. 137). Consequently, in today's cultural environment, this form of compensation is considered appropriate by many for most professions in the United States.

Until the beginning of the Industrial Revolution, workers' compensation bore little relationship to the amount of work produced. As economics developed as an independent discipline, the concept of "the economic man," a person who would respond to incentives, emerged. "Where wages are high, accordingly we shall always find the workmen more active, diligent, and expeditious than where they are low" (Smith, 1976, Book 1, p. 91).

As the Industrial Revolution proceeded, the use of wage incentives became more common, particularly in labor-intensive types of production (Hopkins, 1992, p. 12). Labor costs are a large proportion of total costs for labor-intensive production processes. Labor costs at higher education institutions represent a majority of total costs, making higher education labor intensive. The late nineteenth century American economist, John Bates Clark, showed that firms wishing to maximize profit should hire labor up to the point where the monetary value of the last worker's marginal product (extra output) is equal to the wage rate. This theory became known as the marginal productivity theory of income distribution and was endorsed by both employers and employees. This microeconomic principle provides the basic intellectual support for incentive pay, or merit pay as it became known in higher education.

In the twentieth century, the discipline of economics continued to support incentive pay, but another social science, psychology, also published rationales for this compensation system. Economic analysis tends to focus on the benefits for the organization and the market system, while psychological analysis concentrates on why individual humans respond to pay for performance. Table 3 summarizes the twentieth century psychological and economic studies that built on Clark's late nineteenth century work in support of incentive pay. (See Heneman, 1992, pp. 24–43, for a detailed discussion of these twentieth century studies.)

Psychological Theories Supporting Merit Pay

The major psychological theories supporting merit pay are expectancy theory, reinforcement theory, equity theory, and goal setting theory.

Expectancy Theory. Expectancy theory assumes that individuals react to three perceptions in deciding what to do. The *expectancy perception* is the person's belief that a given level of work will result in a certain level of performance. The *instrumentality perception* is that the expected performance will produce a certain outcome. The *valance perception* deals with the attractiveness of outcomes. The individual combines these perceptions in a multiplicative fashion and decides how to act based on the size of the combined outcomes. If a perception has zero value to the individual, the motivation to act is zero. A merit pay system is likely to motivate workers if the following characteristics are present in the system:

1. Performance is accurately measured.
2. Increased pay is a valued outcome.
3. The performance and pay relationship is clearly defined.
4. Opportunities to improve performance exist.

Reinforcement Theory. A theory that builds on B. F. Skinner's research on operant conditioning (popularly known as behaviorism) is reinforcement theory, which argues that individual behavior is the result of the consequences of different behaviors. In other words, with respect to human behavior, "the best way to get something done is to provide a reward to people when they act the way we want them to" (Kohn, 1993a, p. 3). Empirical research on the effectiveness of pay for performance "suggests that when the principles of

TABLE 3
Implications for Effective Merit Compensation Systems

1. Changes in performance must be accurately measured.

2. Employees must value the increased compensation that is a consequence of performance.

3. The relationship between performance and compensation increases must be clearly defined.

   - Increased compensation must be contingent upon improved performance.

   - Size of reward must be directly related to size of improvement in performance.

   - All factors (both internal and external) that influence the size of the reward must be clearly delineated.

   - All details of the merit plan must be clearly communicated.

   - Merit awards should be based on specific goals.

   - Both goals and rewards should be discussed simultaneously with employees.

4. Receipt of the reward should closely follow the improved performance.

5. Decision makers should realize that individual rewards are not independent of those of others.

6. Employees' perceptions about the relationship between performance and rewards are as important as the actual awards.

7. Size of the award should be based on the difficulty of the improved performance.

8. Size of merit awards should not be any greater than the value of the worker's marginal product.

9. Merit awards should be aligned with what competitors are paying their employees.

10. If the general pay scale is relatively low, merit awards are more important than for employees working in an occupation with a relatively high general pay scale.

11. Implementation of a merit system should reduce the amount of time managers spend monitoring employees and put the burden on employees.

reinforcement theory are followed, performance is indeed increased as pre-dicted from the theory" (Heneman, 1992, p. 29). The use of reinforcement theory to determine merit pay has several implications:

1. Desired improvements in performance must be clearly delineated.
2. The reward must be contingent on the desired improvement in performance.
3. The size of the reward must be directly related to the level of performance improvement.
4. The granting of the reward should be chronologically close to the improvement in performance.

Equity Theory. Equity theory argues that a successful pay-for-performance compensation system depends on the reward the individual receives and its position relative to rewards received by other people with whom the individual compares her/himself. This theory assumes that people compare their own outcomes (financial and other forms of rewards) to inputs to the outcomes/input ratio of others. If the individual believes that others are being rewarded relatively better, the individual feels underrewarded. If the individual believes others are being rewarded relatively worse, a feeling of overreward develops. In both situations, the individual alters inputs in an attempt to restore equity. It can be argued that an individual increases or decreases his/her own inputs if there is a feeling of inequity, so the theory does not predict specific individual behavior. A successful merit plan based on equity theory has several implications:

1. Individual decisions about merit pay are not independent of those of others.
2. The factors that determine rewards for performance must be clearly delineated.
3. Details of merit pay plans must be clearly communicated to employees.
4. Employees' perceptions of the relationship between performance and reward are just as important as the actual relationship.

Goal Setting Theory. This theory contends that setting specific goals motivates employees if those goals are challenging and accepted by employees. This argument outlines the characteristics of goals used in a merit compensation system. Goals should be challenging but not impossible, specific not general, and everyone should accept the goals. This theory does not have much empirical research to support it, but the theory does provide some useful characteristics of successful merit systems:

1. Merit rewards should be based on specific goals.
2. The size of the reward should be based on the level of the goal's difficulty as well as achievement of the goal.
3. Both goals and rewards should be discussed simultaneously.

Economic Theories Supporting Merit Pay

In addition to the psychological theories supporting merit pay, a number of economic theories support it: marginal productivity theory, implicit contract theory, and efficiency wage theory.

Marginal Productivity Theory. As mentioned, this economic interpretation originated with John Bates Clark in 1888. It is profitable for a firm to hire labor up to the point where the value of its marginal product equals the wage rate. To a firm, paying according to value of marginal product is beneficial because it gives workers incentive to produce more, it attracts those who are willing to work hard, and it reduces the chance of a capable worker's leaving the firm. Even though empirical research indicates that firms in reality do not pay wages linked exactly to the value of marginal product, the theory does have relevance for a successful merit system:

1. Marginal productivity of the individual worker must be measured carefully.
2. The theory provides an upper limit on merit awards; they must not be greater than the value of marginal product.

Implicit Contract Theory. This theory originated to address two problems in the assumptions of marginal productivity theory: that labor units are homogeneous and that performance can be accurately measured. In reality, labor is heterogeneous, and marginal productivity is often difficult to measure objectively. A complicating realistic factor is that one worker's performance is often influenced by external factors beyond his or her control. To avoid impacts on performance of overpay and underpay, it is more efficient to set up a contract with each worker specifying performance and pay. Some empirical support for this theory exists; it has some implications for a successful merit compensation system:

1. The performance of individual workers must be carefully measured.
2. Merit awards should be adjusted for the presence of external factors that have positive *or* negative impacts on workers' performance.

Efficiency Wage Theory. This theory implies that it is best for a firm to pay a premium wage to guarantee that employees perform at their maximum. The premium wage would have a ceiling equal to the value of marginal product. If a premium wage is paid, the employer will find that turnover is reduced, the quality of applicants for employment is enhanced, there is less shirking of responsibility by employees, and there is less need for monitoring workers' performance. All these factors reduce the overall cost of labor. Empirical support for this theory is minimal because it is a recent development. Nevertheless, it has some implications for a successful merit system:

1. Employers should consider what competitors are paying their employees and keep wages in alignment with what they are paying.
2. For low wage employers, merit awards are more important than they are in high wage industries.
3. Merit pay should result in employees' monitoring their own performance better.

Table 3 summarizes implications from psychology and economics for a successful merit system.

Arguments Supporting a Single Salary System

Fewer arguments in the literature on faculty compensation support a single salary schedule for faculty than support merit pay. The reason for this difference is not clear, but it could result from a difference in the complexity of the two compensation systems. The published arguments in support of a single salary schedule center around fairness and equity (Hansen, 1988, p. 13; Beaumont, 1978, p. 19).

The rationale among some faculty members who believe that a single salary schedule is fair or equitable can be summarized as "equal pay for equal work." The implicit assumption is that all faculty are equal in terms of their quality and productivity. At a more theoretical level, a single salary schedule can be viewed as adhering to "the classic Aristotelian view that equity in organizations or social groups is achieved through proportionality, or at least ordinal consistency . . . [which] means that organizations should pursue both 'horizontal' and 'vertical' equity in the ways they treat their employees. Horizontal equity is exhibited by rewarding those of equal worth to an organization equally. Vertical equity is exhibited by rewarding people of greater worth to an organization more generously than those of less worth to the organization" (Hearn, 1999, p. 397).

An institution with a strict single salary schedule with no variation in compensation from faculty member to faculty member can be interpreted as abiding by horizontal equity alone. Some would likely criticize such an institution for not attempting to reward those faculty who are worth more to the institution to achieve vertical equity. Under a faculty compensation system that most faculty believe produces "greater fairness," a number of alleged beneficial operational characteristics emerge (Hansen, 1988, p. 13), discussed in the next section.

Operational Advantages and Disadvantages of the Faculty Compensation Systems

IN ADDITION to the intellectual arguments favoring one type of faculty compensation system over another, each type of system has its own advantages and disadvantages when used by an institution of higher education. They are more pragmatic than the theoretical reasons to adopt one compensation system over another. Which of these pragmatic issues is relevant for a particular institution depends on that institution's history, culture, and future goals and objectives. The literature on faculty compensation has numerous articles that deal with practical advantages and disadvantages of different systems. Use of a system in the real world with real faculty can often generate unexpected results. This section first examines faculty merit compensation systems, then single salary systems, and finally alternative systems.

Operational Advantages of Merit Compensation Systems

The operational reasons to support a merit faculty compensation system "are directed, for the most part, at the overall goals of a given institution rather than toward specific situations" (Fassiotto, 1986, p. 6). From this viewpoint, support for a merit faculty compensation system in higher education could have its foundation in the belief that such a system represents characteristics the institution wishes to represent regardless of the impact on individual faculty behavior. This contention implies that the actual relative impacts of a merit system on faculty teaching, scholarly activity, and professional service may be of secondary importance to the institutional image such a compensation system exhibits to society.

Research suggests that administrators typically perceive merit compensation for faculty in positive terms (Brewer, Brewer, and Hilton, 1990, p. 55), while faculty often perceive such systems in negative terms. In other words, "merit pay is embraced by administrators but mistrusted by faculty" (Barnett, Cohen, Jeffries, and Rosen, 1988, p. 19). This difference of opinion likely results from a difference in perspective because "salaries [are viewed] as a means for administrators to reinforce behavioral norms" (Fairweather, 1995, p. 180).

While administrators look at faculty compensation from an institutional perspective, faculty are more concerned with intrusions in their activities. In essence, academic administrators can be expected to emphasize the positive impact on institutional characteristics, while faculty can be expected to focus on unwanted intrusions. If there are both general positive benefits and specific negative costs to a merit compensation system in a higher education institution, the question for academic decision makers should be whether the extra benefits outweigh the extra costs or vice versa. If an institution adopts a merit compensation system because of positive external appearances, there must be congruence between the philosophy behind the compensation system and its actual implementation. Otherwise, faculty anger and resentment over compensation will result, causing a decrease in morale and distrust of the administration.

The operational reasons favoring a merit system follow:

- *Rewarding more productive faculty gives incentives to other faculty to improve their own productivity* (Guzzo, Jette, and Katzell, 1985, p. 289). This assertion rests on two implicit assumptions: that humans are motivated to do better by financial incentives and that faculty are also financially motivated.
- *Merit increases motivate individual faculty to strive for excellence* (Osif and Harwood, 1995, p. 244). This reason focuses on the same aspect of faculty behavior as the first reason; however, a third implicit assumption appears. Presumably, an individual striving for excellence would increase productivity only if rewarded. This statement implies that faculty who do not work in a merit system institution are satisfied with something less than

excellence. Evidence to counter this third implication was observed recently in the California State University system when a merit faculty pay system was adopted in the system in place of a single salary schedule: "the [meritorious] evaluations that resulted in the awards were based on work these faculty had completed over the previous two years when no merit incentives were in place. Obviously, many faculty already were performing 'outstanding and meritorious service to the California State University system' without monetary incentives to spur them on. Perhaps this faculty success resulted from the freedom to be creative, to collaborate, and to trust what they felt was important about their work. . . ." (Hammond and McDermott, 1997, p. 108).

- *A merit compensation system can be used to raise the average institutional salary* (Fassiotto, 1986, p. 7). It has been asserted that "faculties at merit-system colleges tend, on the average, to earn more than those at non-merit-system colleges" (p. 7). This situation will actually occur if one or more faculty "superstars" earn significantly higher compensation than they would under a single salary schedule.

- *Communication and feedback between an individual faculty member and administrators are improved under a merit compensation system* (Clardy, 1988). This institutional advantage stems from a common opinion among administrators that "if they have leverage over the reward system, they can influence behavior" (Lauer, 1991, p. 54). Presumably, faculty who did not receive a merit increase would visit with the administrator to find out what he or she can do to increase performance.

- *Merit compensation systems are politically attractive because they portend to align themselves with the tenets of free enterprise* (Lauer, 1991, p. 54; Johnson, 1984b, p. 24; Calhoun, 1983, p. 1). "The concept of merit pay for teachers embraces a fundamental American ethic: workers should be paid on the basis of their skills and performance" (Calhoun, 1983, p. 1). Thus, merit systems in the present political climate represent a politically acceptable reason to adopt such a compensation system at an institution of higher education.

- *A merit compensation system would give faculty who are highly productive and successful incentive to remain in higher education while giving unproductive faculty incentive to leave* (Johnson, 1984b, p. 24). This argument implicitly assumes that without merit compensation, the total reward for faculty, including monetary and nonmonetary benefits, is less than they could realize outside academia.

- *Merit compensation reduces the incentive for faculty to search for and acquire second jobs outside the institution to supplement their income* (Fassiotto, 1986, p. 7). This statement could be true for individual faculty whose compensation increases more rapidly than average under a merit system.

- *Merit compensation can boost faculty morale* (Hunnicutt, Taylor and Keeffe 1991, p. 19). A merit compensation system established with input from faculty, administered objectively and fairly, and providing compensation increments that reflect economic realities could boost faculty morale. Unfortunately, such a system may be difficult to set up and negotiate over time.

- *For institutions that adopt a faculty merit compensation system, administrators will experience greater management discretion by being able to reward faculty behaviors that the administration endorses, that is, "discriminately distribute merit pay"* (Miller, 1992, p. 9). Administrative discretion, in its most general sense, implies that administrators are privy to information that enables them to choose the optimal from alternative courses of action so as to maximize the public's interest (Fox and Cochran, 1990, p. 249). Substitute "the institution's interest" for "the public's interest" in the previous sentence to apply it to higher education administrators.

- *Institutions with a faculty merit compensation system "where annual salary increases reward merit, will have greater ease in attracting top quality faculty, and particularly researchers, from institutions with structured salary systems"* (Hansen, 1988, p. 12). This institutional advantage appeals to external faculty currently employed at institutions using a single salary schedule whose output is recognized as meritorious, because it provides a financial attraction in the form of "potential for above-average salary increases based on the high quality of their performance and the favorable merit assessments they can expect to receive" (Hansen, 1988, p. 12). In other words, high quality faculty tend to move into institutions with faculty merit compensation systems.

Operational Disadvantages of Merit Compensation Systems

The literature on faculty compensation lists several operational disadvantages of using merit faculty compensation systems, primarily because of their impact on individual faculty behavior. Some of these operational disadvantages have been cited in reports about nontraditional compensation systems.

- *Faculty merit compensation systems may not increase faculty productivity because of the distinctive nature of faculty work* (Tharp, 1991, p. 75) *or may not actually motivate faculty* (Hunnicutt, Taylor, and Keeffe, 1991, p. 20). Some argue that higher education has a "distinctive collegial environment where merit pay can have an adverse effect on [an] employee's work" (Tharp, 1991, p. 75). Other critics question whether merit pay actually motivates faculty in higher education. A survey study of educational administrators indicated that "merit pay was considered significantly less effective than the other variables in affecting faculty behavior . . . [the administrators sampled] viewed tenure as having a greater effect on faculty behavior than the other variables" (Marchant and Newman, 1994, p. 149). A study from 1991 asserts that "there is a dearth of evidence that merit systems, in practice, actually achieve their primary goal of increasing faculty productivity" (Hunnicutt, Taylor, and Keeffe, 1991, p. 20) and points out that, in 1991, there was no solid evidence to either support or refute the assertion of increased faculty productivity.
- *Most, if not all, evaluative instruments measure quantity and not quality* (Dennis, 1982, p. 20). This problem arises when a merit system is put into place without carefully delineating what should be rewarded: a higher quantity of output with less quality or less output of higher quality. This factor, coupled with professional scholarship's being easier to measure than teaching effectiveness or professional service, generates complaints of "trivial scholarship" with little extra value to society (Mooney, 1991, p. A1). Because faculty under merit systems quickly determine what counts and what does not, institutions must use care in developing the system to ensure alignment with the institution's mission.

- *Subjective decisions are more likely with a merit compensation system than with a single salary schedule* (Hooker, 1978; Fassiotto, 1986, p. 18; Hunnicutt, Taylor, and Keeffe, 1991, p. 19). Faculty receiving merit compensation "may be superior performers, but more likely than not, they will have charismatic personalities that attract students, parents, and administrators. . . . [Faculty] job descriptions make no mention of charisma, yet often charisma is the determining factor in selecting recipients of merit pay" (Gilchrist and White, 1990, p. 249).

  Similarly, "physical proximity to the chairman's office is essential" (Hooker, 1978, p. 48). In other words, having an office next to the chair's office will greatly increase the probability of receiving merit increases. Any compensation system with different increments awarded to different individuals may reflect decisions based on subjective or nonobjective criteria.

- *Developing a fair system is difficult* (Fassiotto, 1986, p. 12). The evolution of salary structures for workers in the United States resulted in two somewhat diametrically opposed viewpoints currently held. One notes that merit systems are politically attractive and consistent with the tenets of free enterprise. Over the last one hundred years, however, the union movement has encouraged "the belief that all employees on the same job should be treated the same" (Miller, 1992, p. 9). Consequently, many workers, including faculty in higher education, believe that a single salary system is fairer than a merit system.

  A study analyzing the attitudes of faculty at a midwestern state university toward various aspects of merit compensation revealed that only 16 percent of the respondents believed a total merit compensation system "would enhance their sense of the fairness of salary decisions" (Wood and Burke, 1989, p. 11).

- *The relationship between performance and compensation is weak* (Hammond and McDermott, 1997, p. 108; Lauer, 1991, pp. 52–53; Calhoun, 1983, p. 10). A close link between an individual's improved performance and a merit reward is a requisite for making a merit system effective. The inability to perceive a direct link between performance and pay has been cited as a critical problem with any pay-for-performance compensation system. To achieve a strong motivational effect with a merit compensation system, two things must be present: (1) a short period of time between the improved performance and the receipt of the reward, and (2) a significant increase in compensation for a strongly performing worker. The nature of faculty work, the frequency and timing of salary adjustments for faculty, and the size and inconsistency of increases in institutional funding militate against a strong motivational effect for merit systems in higher education.

Still another factor reducing the relationship between performance and reward is "the presence of uncertainty or ambiguity in the evaluation and salary-determination process" (Konrad and Pfeffer, 1990, p. 260). Three factors have been identified as contributing to uncertainty and ambiguity in higher education faculty merit compensation systems. "The first factor is unclear or ambiguous criteria for evaluating performance. Second, the nature of the social relations among faculty members, and specifically, the degree of contact and interdependence, can affect how clearly both performance and the normative structure of the pay-allocation process are known. Finally, consistent with some of the research on the effect of secrecy, factors that affect the ambiguity of pay allocation resulting from differences in governance that make evaluation and salary allocations more or less open will affect the pay-performance relationship" (Konrad and Pfeffer, 1990, p. 261).

- *Collegiality, collaboration, and cohesiveness among faculty decrease; divisiveness, distrust, and jealously increase* (Hammond and McDermott, 1997, pp. 107–108). A faculty merit compensation system can generate suspicion and hostility among faculty, particularly where criteria and procedures are not clearly defined (Miller, 1992, p. 9). This problem has two parts: the first may occur with a carefully constructed and fairly administered merit compensation system, while the second could occur with a system that has no clearly defined criteria and procedures.

The problem that can exist even with a well constructed and administered system occurs if faculty view merit compensation as a zero-sum game. In this case, it would likely lead to divisiveness, distrust, and jealously among the employees involved. Such a situation would occur if the system has a finite quota of meritorious awards or a finite amount of funds available for increases in compensation. Institutions of higher education typically experience the second situation. Consequently, "merit can . . . erode collegiality and create excessive competition" (Miller, 1992, p. 9). A survey of faculty attitudes about merit compensation indicates that "few believed that merit systems would promote cooperation among faculty colleagues" (Wood and Burke, 1989, p. 14).

- *The relative importance of teaching effectiveness and service activities to individual faculty members decreases* (Hammond and McDermott, 1997, p. 111; Hunnicutt, Taylor, and Keeffe, 1991, p. 19; Brewer, Brewer, and Hilton, 1990, p. 52). This pragmatic problem with faculty merit pay is often stated in the literature and during personal conversations among faculty. The cause stems from the fact that effective teaching and service can be evaluated only in subjective terms while faculty tend to prefer objective evaluations. The various disciplines have a long history of evaluating scholarly research and publication, making it easy for merit evaluations to focus on a faculty member's number of professional publications and making the reward for research and publication higher and more definite than rewards for teaching and service.

Because published scholarship is a common element of merit compensation plans and is easy to measure, faculty working under a merit system are given incentive to switch from concentrating on effective teaching to scholarship after the imposition of a merit system (Hammond and McDermott, 1997, p. 111; Hunnicutt, Taylor, and Keeffe, 1991, p. 19; Brewer, Brewer, and Hilton, 1990, p. 52). In a 1989 survey of 85 college of business deans to determine what factors are used to promote research productivity in the southeastern portion of the United States, 97.6 percent of the "responding deans [believed] that the presence of a merit pay system can and/or does increase faculty research productivity" (Brewer, Brewer, and Hilton, 1990, p. 54).

The third traditional component of faculty activity and the one given least weight in most compensation systems is service, either institutional or professional. Faculty advance two reasons for the low value attributed to service activities: "Public service is so loosely defined that profession-related and non-profession-related services are not distinguished from one another [and] because good measures of professional public service do not exist, it is difficult to distinguish the excellent from the good, the good from the mediocre, or the mediocre from the poor" (Florestano and Hambrick, 1984, p. 18). Because service "is not well rewarded in most university environments, . . . this absence of reward prevents the full development of outreach programs" (p. 18). An institution with a stated element of its mission as providing professional service to its community or region needs to carefully construct a faculty merit system that includes meaningful rewards to faculty who do engage in professional service.

- *The quality of scholarship decreases while quantity increases* (Hansen, 1988, p. 13). A common criticism of merit compensation systems in higher education is "too great a focus upon quantity instead of quality" (Wood and Wood, 1988, p. 10), causing faculty to "avoid complex research problems in favor of simple problems more likely to result in reward" (Burke, 1988, p. 6). Thus, under a merit compensation system, faculty may pursue a "minimax" strategy by choosing "less difficult and challenging tasks to assure rewards, reducing the overall quality of performance among faculty" (Hunnicutt, Taylor, and Keeffe, 1991, p. 15). This phenomenon has been observed in industrial workplaces that have a merit compensation system in place.

- *Productivity will be decreased if faculty perceive an unfairly administered system or one that does not differentiate among faculty in a meaningful way* (Renner and Jester, 1980, p. 161). Moreover, a merit system may be carefully constructed and faculty fairly evaluated yet have operational problems in practice and may "not automatically lead to improvements in organizational performance" (Gilchrist and White, 1990, p. 249). This operational problem has two parts.

The first problem results from a characteristic of faculty work often not taken into account; that is, an individual faculty member has limited opportunity to adjust his or her work effort in response to perceived problems in the compensation system. For example, if a faculty member's real income falls over time, it is possible that less time will be spent on teaching, research, and service. In a survey of faculty at a large southeastern university during a time of rising compensation, "almost half (43 percent) reported a decline in their effort to do a good job. In contrast only 7 percent reported that they were trying to do better" (Renner and Jester, 1980, pp. 160–161).

Second, even a carefully constructed and fairly administered faculty merit compensation system may have operational problems in practice and may cause the institution's general performance to decrease. If faculty collegiality, collaboration, and cohesiveness decrease because of the presence of a merit compensation system, the institution's general performance decreases.

> **If faculty collegiality, collaboration, and cohesiveness decrease because of the presence of a merit compensation system, the institution's general performance decreases.**

- *Do college faculty who are highly qualified professionals need to be closely scrutinized?* (Elliott and Ryan, 1986, p. 129). Granting differing levels of compensation on the basis of differing levels of performance requires a considerable amount of reporting by faculty members. This reporting could have the effect of leading faculty to believe that administrators do not trust faculty to perform on their own. Undoubtedly, many faculty feel insulted by being forced to report on their activities to administration, even with a carefully constructed and fairly administered merit compensation system.

- *It takes an inordinate amount of time to compile data for evaluative measures* (Taylor, Hunnicutt, and Keeffe, 1991, p. 65; Lauer, 1991, p. 54), because "the process of evaluation inevitably involves much form-filling; if a form is not used, some standardized means of self-reporting will usually be required. . . . Thus, those most adept at form-filling (or those who take most time away from other professional duties to do it) are those, ipso facto, who present the most convincing briefs on their own behalf" (Dennis, 1982, p. 19).

The use of a merit system to determine faculty compensation represents another bureaucratic process that involves decision-making committees and time-consuming paperwork for an institution. A merit system adds to the amount of paperwork faculty members must produce and administrators must read.

- *Evaluation systems tend to focus on the extremes of high and low performance, and evaluators may overlook the contributions of individuals who, while not top rated, are strong and consistent performers* (Magnusen, 1987, p. 525). The majority of work in an organization comes from individuals in the middle of the performance hierarchy; consequently, merit systems designed to reward high performers may not really motivate this large cadre of workers: "the people companies really have to motivate are the middle group of solid performers. If they can increase performance at that level, they're going to get more leverage overall" (Kitsuse, 1992, p. 24). Even though this comment is directed at profit-making business firms, it has relevance to institutions of higher education or to any organization with a majority of solid performers and relatively few superstars.

- *Merit systems tend to focus on individual performance while ignoring joint or team efforts* (Chait, 1988, p. 23). The productivity of an institution of higher education is often the result of a team effort. "Almost without exception, teachers, scholars, and administrators are compensated, promoted, and otherwise rewarded for *individual* performance; rarely, if ever, do colleges and universities reward *collective* performance. In fact, on many campuses the incentive structure discourages collegial behavior" (p. 23). Moreover, "the process whereby individuals and groups of professors labor to produce 'knowledge' through their collegial interactions, research, teaching, and administrative duties appears so bewilderingly complex as to defy any reasoned effort to define, much less measure the specific contribution made by any individual faculty member" (Elliott and Ryan, 1986, p. 133).

- *With a merit system, a struggle arises between the administration, which wants to allocate rewards on the basis of performance, and faculty, who seem, somehow perversely, to prefer a less proportional allocation of salary* (Konrad and Pfeffer, 1990, p. 279). This difference of attitude could result from "a business ethos [in academic administration that] has supplanted the value orientation of the scholar. . . . Faculties, however, have not given up their guild [of scholars] orientation" (Counelis, 1984, pp. 4–7). In other words, to institutional administrators, merit compensation increases for faculty are analogous to commissions paid to a retail store's best salesperson, the one with the largest number of sales. Faculty, however, view merit compensation increases to reflect an individual faculty member's esteem relative to colleagues. Consequently, if a faculty merit compensation system results in most institutional faculty receiving merit increases, the faculty in general may view the system as rewarding the wrong types of faculty output.

- *If awards are added to base compensation, the system becomes very costly over time* (Kitsuse, 1992, p. 24). Some institutional merit compensation systems add the annual award to base salary instead of granting a one-time stipend. Consequently, "even a small increase in pay adds up to a lot of money over time, because base-salary increases are an annuity" (p. 24).

How faculty merit compensation systems impact institutional budgets receives little discussion in the literature and thus constitutes a viable future research topic. The reason for this paucity of discussion in the literature may be that institutions adopt merit systems for reasons other than what it will cost; consequently, institutions give little thought to this topic.

- *Offering extrinsic merit rewards "may interfere with performance for the sake of self-satisfaction"* (Bassett, 1994, p. 21) *or intrinsic motivation.* Faculty in higher education are often described as becoming faculty for intrinsic reasons: self-satisfaction from educating students, engaging in meaningful research, or providing useful service. Merit compensation represents an extrinsic motivating factor; "various studies have demonstrated that when emphasis is put on pay as a motivator of task performance, a worker's sense of intrinsic task interest may diminish. . . . Being paid a little below market may, in some instances, be offset by an enhanced sense of intrinsic interest in the job. Emphasis on 'pay for performance' may interfere with performance for the sake of self-satisfaction" (p. 21).

- *Some university professors are opposed to the merit system because they feel that the system violates their academic freedom* (Elliott and Ryan, 1986, p. 129). A merit compensation system is nothing but a reward structure designed to encourage certain behaviors. Once in place, a merit compensation system causes the individual faculty member to lose some autonomy in terms of deciding how to educate students, engage in research, or perform professional service. The monetary reward gives faculty incentive to pursue only those activities that can most easily obtain the reward; consequently, academic freedom of individual faculty members decreases.

- *Some argue that a merit system has a political weakness because funds designated for merit increases in state-supported institutions may be chosen to reduce state expenditures* (Lauer, 1991, p. 53). This issue pertains more to institutions with cost of living faculty compensation increases stated as merit increases. Consequently, state-supported institutions are in a no win situation. The state legislature may demand that all faculty compensation increases be merit based, and if an institution refers to a cost of living increase as base merit, the state legislature may view such funds as unnecessary.

- *Publication of merit awards is necessary to verify system credibility, which may be contrary to the campus culture at some institutions* (Lauer, 1991, p. 53). "In true merit pay systems, the winners are known. Top producers are announced, their names are put on plaques, and their achievements are touted. Merit systems are competitive by nature. Colleges and universities are collegial. If an institution is not willing to publicize merit producers, the system will be suspect" (p. 53). Further, keeping the meritorious faculty and the amounts of the awards secret undermines the provision of incentives to less productive faculty. Despite these points, many institutions keep the names of recipients and the amounts of merit awards secret. Presumably, secrecy is maintained to avoid discomfort to merit award recipients, which consequently may create larger problems elsewhere and may not be worth it.

- *Some faculty argue that a faculty compensation system should not be used to financially punish individual faculty members.* If insufficient funds are available to grant a cost of living adjustment to all faculty, awarding merit increases only to meritorious faculty could be perceived as punishment by faculty who do not receive increases (Miller, 1992, p. 9). In other words, "to be effective, merit pay needs to be at least two times the average increment. . . . Designating [cost of living] money as merit pay in effect punishes employees who do not receive an increase above the cost of living. This is sometimes called (de)merit pay" (Lauer, 1991, p. 53). The punishment effect becomes more significant when insufficient funds are available to award a cost of living adjustment to every faculty member who is performing satisfactorily and the institution awards extraordinary merit awards to a select few faculty.

- *Faculty would likely object if institutional administration uses a faculty merit compensation system to "discriminately distribute merit pay"* (Miller, 1992, p. 9) *only to faculty who behave in a fashion approved by the administration.* Managers outside academia often "discriminately distribute merit pay" to employees performing in a fashion approved by management. Faculty in higher education would find such administrative discretion distasteful, however, because "traditionally faculty members in higher education have functioned in their roles without a great deal of regard for how their performance would be evaluated and compensated. However, declining enrollments and decreased public funding for education have forced university administrators and the faculty to be more accountable for the cost of quality education. One method used to encourage faculty accountability is the merit system for allocation of salary increases. . . . Many persons in academe have felt that the merit system is just a means by which administrators can exert tight control over faculty" (Elliott and Ryan, 1986, p. 129). In other words, a faculty merit compensation system has become "a tool to increase the autocratic power of each institution's president at the expense of the faculty and its union" (Hammond and McDermott, 1997, p. 107).

- *Institutions that focus on merit are more likely to neglect the compensation of temporary and part-time faculty and graduate students.* "When pay policy begins with cost-of-living adjustments and across-the-board increases for satisfactory performance, it usually includes some provision for all employees. Non-tenure-track faculty are rarely expected and often are not fully eligible to participate in the research life of the university, and they may drop out of consideration when merit rules. Like its football team, the university relies upon 'walk-ons' to complete the teaching roster but gives its rewards to the 'money players' (Pratt, 1988, p. 16). This situation occurs because if an institution has a finite source of funds for faculty compensation, a zero-sum game results: if one faculty member or one group receives a larger compensation increase, some other faculty member or faculty group must receive a smaller one. Because non-tenure-track faculty and graduate students stay a short time at the institution, their interests can be of less concern to the institution.

Operational Advantages of Single Salary Systems

Some faculty support a single salary system for faculty compensation based on a theoretical or philosophical rationale of fairness or equity. A single salary schedule, in contrast to a merit faculty compensation system, turns the basis for compensation from performance to longevity and survivorship. "By de-emphasizing competition, it might be argued, these institutions foster greater collegiality and better morale, lead to deeper levels of scholarship, and relieve the pressure to publish regularly while emphasizing quality teaching" (Hansen, 1988, p. 13).

In addition to these four advantages (greater collegiality, higher faculty morale, deeper level of scholarship, and quality teaching), a single salary schedule generates a more stable and long-lasting faculty, has no impact on the level of faculty teamwork (Foldesi, 1996, p. 29), and represents a compensation system that is easy to administer (Beaumont, 1978, p. 19).

- *A single salary system promotes greater collegiality and cooperation among different faculty members* (Hansen, 1988, p. 13). Collegiality means different things to different individuals in higher education, but with respect to faculty compensation, it can likely be taken as shared authority among colleagues. Authority in this context means that the level of compensation does not distinguish higher performing individuals among a collegiate faculty. In other words, each faculty member has the same level of authority as measured by compensation except for differences in levels of experience. Further, there would be no individual feelings of inadequacy or inferiority among faculty who earn a lower compensation level than a colleague.

  Collegiality can also be manifested in greater cooperation among faculty members. If a single salary schedule does in fact result in greater cooperation among faculty, it is a worthwhile characteristic. It is reasonable to conclude that, under a performance based faculty compensation system, faculty members purposely do not cooperate with colleagues because it may result in a difference in merit awards.

- *A single salary system promotes higher faculty morale* (Hansen, 1988, p. 13). The impact on faculty morale of a single salary schedule relates to the objective measures used to determine compensation levels. A faculty member's degree of educational achievement and years of experience are objective measures that are readily observable by other faculty, so the specific reason for a particular faculty member's compensation is objective. Some critics of performance based faculty compensation systems claim that subjective criteria are used to determine compensation levels, because objective measures of some dimensions of faculty performance are not possible. With a strict single salary schedule, there would be little chance for suspicion in the minds of some faculty that other faculty are being improperly favored because there is less opportunity for subjective evaluation of a faculty member's worth to the institution. Consequently, faculty morale may be higher.

Another possible boost to faculty morale by a single salary schedule is that the greatest degree of faculty autonomy arguably is possible with such a schedule. In a faculty merit compensation system, specific activities can be favored and rewarded by administrators, resulting in less faculty autonomy. Consequently, with a single salary schedule, faculty have more protection from administrative manipulation and control. In other words, there is less administrative managerial discretion under a single salary schedule, which should improve faculty morale.

- *A single salary schedule promotes a deeper level of scholarship* (Hansen, 1988, p. 13). A single salary schedule has been cited as promoting higher quality and more rigorous scholarship because faculty no do not have to worry about surviving in a "publish or perish" environment where the quantity of published scholarship may be the important variable (p. 13). In other words, faculty can be free to examine a scholastic topic more definitively because there is no pressure to "hurry up and publish a paper this year" just to acquire a merit award.

- *A single salary schedule emphasizes high-quality teaching* (Hansen, 1988, p. 13). A single salary schedule possibly could cause faculty to concentrate more on effective teaching. Surveys of faculty in higher education usually find that a large proportion of faculty prefer teaching. "When asked about various academic responsibilities, four in ten faculty report that they are primarily interested in teaching, which is about seven times the number primarily interested in research. The rest are equally interested in teaching and research, with slightly more claiming a preference for the former over the latter" (Lewis, 1996, p. 28). Institutions whose missions primarily emphasize quality teaching may find it appropriate to have a single salary schedule or a combined single salary schedule and merit compensation system.

- *The stability and longevity of the faculty are enhanced and promoted* (Foldesi, 1996, p. 29). Critics would argue that this outcome occurs because of the nature of the compensation system and, as such, represents a negative.

- *A single salary schedule does not "overtly diminish teamwork because everybody gets the same relative increase; conversely, there is no incentive to work effectively as a team member"* (Foldesi, 1996, p. 29). An institution concerned about promoting teamwork among faculty may find this point a disadvantage of a single salary schedule.

- *A single salary schedule promotes ease of operation and administration* (Beaumont, 1978, p. 19). A definite advantage for both faculty and administrators of a single salary schedule is the ease of administration. "Equity and ease of administration provide a rationale for the single salary schedule" (p. 19). Once the salary matrix is set up and everyone understands it, determining the salary of every faculty member in the upcoming pay period requires simply a mechanical process of locating the appropriate cell in the salary matrix. For some institutions, this attribute could be a primary one to justify adopting a single salary schedule. Besides administrative simplicity, a single salary schedule "is an administrative dream" (Clardy, 1988, p. 8) for three reasons: (1) Future funding requirements can be predicted fairly accurately, depending on the demographic makeup of the faculty; (2) every faculty member receives the same increase in compensation, so any individual feelings of subjective differences are not a problem; and (3) administrative costs would be kept down by avoiding monitoring of faculty.

Operational Disadvantages of Single Salary Systems

The primary operational problems with a single salary schedule include a lack of efficiency in the use of human resources and the related problem that it rewards an improper faculty attribute–longevity (Beaumont, 1978, p. 19).

Some faculty are displeased with a single salary schedule: "This is the origin of quarrels and complaints when either equals have and are awarded unequal shares, or unequals equal shares. Further, this is plain from the fact that awards should be 'according to merit'; for all men agree that what is just in distribution must be according to merit in some sense, though *they do not all specify the same sort of merit"* [emphasis added] (Aristotle, 1998, p. 112).

In other words, individual faculty have differing views on what constitutes merit or inequality among faculty. Those who believe educational preparation and experience constitute differences among faculty will prefer a single salary schedule, while those who believe something else makes for differences among faculty will prefer a merit pay system that rewards activity in another area.

Operational Advantages of Nontraditional Systems

Institutions that have reported on their experience with nontraditional faculty compensation systems typically cite one or more of the operational disadvantages of using a merit or a single salary compensation system.

Faculty Self-Development Review

This suggestion begins with the contention "that measurable objectives assume a structured work place, which is not compatible with the academic enterprise" (Tharp, 1991, p. 76). In other words, basing merit awards on inaccurate or subjective measures of faculty work can reduce faculty productivity and result in bitterness and low morale. In this view, increasing faculty productivity requires changing faculty evaluations to emphasize growth and self-development and changing the compensation system to make it "rooted in the traditions and organization climate of the institution" (pp. 77–78) so as to attain faculty satisfaction. Such a compensation system gives individual faculty incentive to improve themselves in a way aligned with the mission of the institution.

Single Salary Combined with Merit Increases

The operational advantages typically cited for a combination system include rewarding faculty performing at a satisfactory level and creating stable expectations among the faculty. For example, the step system used in California "has worked well . . . [with] reasonable expectations and fairly uniform treatment of the faculty. It also appears to contain adequate flexibility to reward outstanding accomplishment and to provide members of the faculty with incentives throughout their careers" (Manaster, 1985, p. 26).

Contract Merit System

The contract merit system used at Eastern Washington University was established because "when applied to professional endeavors, merit pay systems should also encourage self-directed activity, since the true professional educator is primarily motivated by personal, nonmonetary rewards, e.g., self-esteem, peer recognition, or student approval. [EWU's] merit pay system helps educators satisfy these needs while simultaneously rewarding achievement of selected goals. In [the university's] experience, the merit pay system has spurred an overall staff development effort of significant proportions. The system operates with a high degree of faculty approval and participation" (Shreeve and others, 1985, p. 155).

The authors cite several advantages of the voluntary merit pay contract system observed in the Department of Education at Eastern Washington University: the system "(1) rewards desired behaviors, (2) individualizes rewards by recognizing diverse attributes and activities, (3) makes merit pay available to all who achieve designated goals, [and] (4) keeps evaluative processes simple and easily administered" (Shreeve and others, 1985, p. 158). All faculty who realize their individualized plans would receive a merit reward. A contract merit compensation system could be combined with a single salary system to provide faculty who are producing at a satisfactory level a compensation increment equal to cost of living increases.

Salary Administration with Merit Compensation

For those faculty concerned about the evaluation of their performance being conducted by one person (the department chair, for instance), with possibilities of personal and nonprofessional prejudices negatively affecting their rating level, Van Fleet points out that no one person determines individual faculty totals with the salary administration and merit system (1972, p. 415).

Further, a salary administration faculty compensation system has several advantages:

> *First, . . . it is developed through joint participation of the major members of the institution. . . . Second, the program recognizes and remunerates all three dimensions of the faculty role rather than relying exclusively on only one or two of those dimensions. Third, the scale would be reasonably objective and it would be known. . . . Fourth, the plan provides continuous pressure on the faculty member to maintain or improve total performance year after year. . . . Fifth, this program rests on the assumption that individuals in higher education . . . are primarily self-motivated and self-controlled. . . . Sixth, the annual performance review would identify the individual's areas of strengths and weaknesses, thus providing him with the information necessary to alter behavior and seek improvement. Furthermore, strong incentives to improve performance would be obtained by defining performance, by tying pay to performance, and by making public both pay and the definitions, scales, and rules surrounding it. (Van Fleet, 1972, p. 417)*

Adjustment for Unjustified Distortions

"Attention on annual increments . . . [in compensation] will allow salary relationships [among faculty] to become distorted by fluctuations in funding levels from year to year" (Clevenger, 1989, p. 8). Difference in subjective evaluation of faculty by administrators represents another source of differences in compensation that could occur. Whatever the source of differences in faculty compensation, an institution that does not address this issue may find faculty morale decreasing. Consequently, periodic adjustments represent a worthwhile policy for any institution to implement, particularly those with a pure merit system but also other institutions with any other compensation system.

Rewards for Faculty Teams

Developing a faculty compensation system that rewards teams has certain operational advantages: "First, the system would bring about more congruity between words and actions [between institutional mission statement and faculty compensation]. . . . Second, . . . group rewards would communicate a clear message about institutional values and desired behavior. Third, the system would link institutional strategies to departmental actions. . . . Finally, . . . [such a system] may actually help faculty members discover or rediscover the intrinsic rewards that derive from collective efforts and collegial activities, especially in an increasingly splintered, fragmented, and specialized profession" (Chait, 1988, p. 24).

Rewards for Professional Public Service

A recent change in the public attitude toward higher education, particularly state-supported institutions, emphasizes more interaction in the form of support for community or regional initiatives. Institutions are being called upon to expand the scope of professional service activity among faculty. Thus, somehow integrating rewards for professional service has become timely and even required by some accrediting agencies.

Requirement for Faculty to Generate Compensation Funds

For most institutions, this nontraditional compensation system could not be used, but for teaching hospitals, dental schools, or veterinary schools, this approach has enough merit to be worth examining.

Designing an Effective Faculty Compensation System

THE FACULTY COMPENSATION SYSTEM a particular higher education institution establishes will have a major impact on the institution's future success and quality. Thus, a plan to establish such a system must be widely discussed and supported before it is implemented. "Designing a compensation system that provides strong incentives for employees to pursue organizational goals is a challenge every organization faces" (Murnane and Cohen, 1986, p. 1).

This section outlines the steps an institution can and should follow in designing and implementing an effective compensation system. An effective faculty compensation system should give individual faculty members an economic motivation to engage in professional activities that work to achieve the institution's mission.

> *Discussions of faculty priorities abound, with a growing number of institutions claiming an increased emphasis on the quality of teaching and on their role in the community. In practice, however, faculty reward systems at these institutions often convey a different emphasis, giving more weight to publications and scholarship than to teaching and community service, thus creating a mixed message for faculty. Disparity between an institution's mission statement and its reward system (what it says and what it does) undercuts the effectiveness of each: If these goals are to be reached, the institution must reward behaviors that best support its mission. (Diamond, 1999, p. ix)*

Research by Neumann and Finaly-Neumann (1990, pp. 75–97) supports the contention that the structure of the faculty reward system impacts the level of success an institution achieves in fulfilling its mission. "Faculty commitment to their university is an essential factor in the process of understanding faculty attitudes, behavior, and effectiveness. . . . The university is expected by faculty members to provide a supportive environment that facilitates the realization of [individual] investments (skills, abilities, and needs) and a work compensation system that is equitable in rewarding these contributions. To the extent that the university is perceived to provide a supportive environment and an equitable reward system, faculty commitment is likely to increase and vice versa" (77–78).

Neumann and Finaly-Neumann's statistical analysis of a random sample of both physical and social science departments at research universities reported that "from a policy perspective, this study calls for different strategies for increasing faculty commitment to their university. In the physical sciences, university central administration ought to emphasize the establishment of clear equity criteria for rewarding faculty members, whereas in the social sciences, faculty commitment is likely to be affected by intrinsic outcomes such as challenge and meaning in work as well as support from a friendly group or from an understanding chairperson" (Neumann and Finaly-Neumann, 1990, p. 93). Further, the authors noted that faculty in applied disciplines such as education and electrical engineering were more highly committed to their university than faculty from nonapplied disciplines such as physics and sociology. The authors hypothesize that the difference in faculty commitment among disciplines occurs because faculty from applied disciplines have the opportunity to chose among more career alternatives than faculty in nonapplied disciplines and consciously make a decision to chose an academic career (p. 93).

Steps to Follow

To develop a faculty compensation system that supports the institutional mission first requires the governing board, president, chief academic officer, or faculty governing body to recognize that the institution should address this issue. The next step is the formation of a committee with a cross section of faculty, administrators, and perhaps students in its membership to examine the issue.

Once formed, the compensation system committee's first task should be to determine how the institution's mission statement in its present form can be used as a guide for developing the compensation system. The assumption is that each institution has a mission statement sensitive to the needs of all stakeholders, including students, faculty, staff, and the public in general, that clearly outlines the institution's vision, values, and goals. "Values are core beliefs that unite members. Vision and values must be communicated throughout the organization in a way that builds commitment and meaning" (Freed, Klugman, and Fife, 1997, p. 55). A clearly articulated institutional mission statement enables individual faculty to obtain guidance about the types of behaviors their institution values. If the compensation system committee feels that the current mission statement does not do so and should be changed, the committee needs to request the appropriate bodies of the institution to develop a mission statement that can be used as the foundation for the faculty compensation system. The compensation system committee should keep in mind throughout the process that an implicit reality of any compensation system is it signals to employees what type of behavior the institution values and rewards. "It is impossible for communication like this not to occur" (Clardy, 1988, p. 7). This communication can be misinterpreted by employees; therefore, it is important to make the compensation system consistent with institutional goals and objectives and to determine how clearly these goals and objectives are communicated.

The committee then should evaluate the existing compensation system and list its strengths and weaknesses in terms of fulfilling the institution's mission. Several questions need to be answered in evaluation of the current compensation system:

> *First, is the system efficient? That is, does it devote an appropriate level of time and other resources to training, communication, and oversight? Second, are the procedures for salary determination equitable? Do affected parties have a role in the process, for example? Third, are the outcomes equitable for those in different fields, for those suffering from the effects of salary compression, for women, and for racial/ethnic minorities? Fourth, is the system well*

understood on campus and, as necessary, beyond the campus? Fifth,
does the system fit with the strategic initiative, management
approach, and organizational culture of the campus? Sixth, does
the system make sense from an internal political perspective? That is,
does it balance the interests of various parties on campus and reflect
current political realities there? Seventh, is the system assessed and
evaluated regularly? (Hearn, 1999, p. 403)

Second, the committee should compile a list of goals and objectives a new system should address. Care should be taken to keep this list short to avoid duplication among goals and objectives. Those compiling the list should provide ample time and opportunity to allow faculty and administrators across the campus to discuss and debate goals and objectives. All the major players on campus should be involved in this discussion to ensure ownership of the resulting system. Table 4 summarizes possible goals a compensation system should strive to reach as found in the literature on faculty compensation.

Even though all these goals are desirable, some may be in conflict, forcing an institution to select only a few. Again, discussion and debate about these goals must be performed at length before implementing any change. Further, an institution should address possible organizational, political, and cultural obstacles to changing the faculty compensation system (Lauer, 1991, p. 52).

Once the strengths and weaknesses of the current compensation system have been determined and the new goals and objectives developed, construction of the new system can begin. Determination of the appropriate general policy the new compensation should follow is the next task. "Specific policy recommendations are rarely appropriate for every institution and, not surprisingly, there are no discernible 'silver bullets' for those interested in salary policy" (Hearn, 1999, pp. 403–404). The literature suggests several policy choices:

Choice 1: Deemphasizing the External Marketplace. . . .
Institutions cannot and should not respond aggressively to changes
in the marketplace, maintaining instead a more locally determined
and presumably more egalitarian approach to salaries.

TABLE 4
Possible Institutional Goals and Objectives
for Faculty Compensation

1. Maintain faculty real purchasing power, equity, and morale.

2. Reward faculty accomplishments aligned with institutional mission and goals.

3. Provide incentives to faculty to change their behavior if needed.

4. Improve faculty performance as defined by the institution.

5. Maintain parity with market to retain and attract faculty in high demand disciplines.

6. Reward faculty for producing benefits to society.

7. Reward collective faculty performance.

8. Retain high quality and productive faculty.

9. Encourage continual improvement by faculty.

10. Provide faculty incentives to develop courses for nontraditional programs of study, such as Internet-based courses.

Choice 2: Adopting the "Core-Salary" Approach. . . . [or] breaking the traditional base salary into a stable "core" component and a second component that is "flexible" or "at risk."

Choice 3: Tying Annual Salary Changes More Directly to Annual Performance [a pure merit system].

Choice 4: Standardizing Salaries in Association with Career Ladders [a single salary system].

Choice 5: Decoupling Merit Evaluation for Salary Increases and Faculty Development Efforts [a faculty self-development review system].

Choice 6: Pursuing Internal Consistency in the Determination of Salaries.

Choice 7: Welcoming Faculty Participation in Determination of Merit-Based Salary Increases.

Choice 8: Facilitating Public Scrutiny of Salaries.
Choice 9: Elevating Teaching and Public Service as Criteria for
Salary Adjustments (Hearn, 1999, pp. 404–407).

Once direction of the institutional general faculty compensation policy has been determined, work can begin on the structure and details of the compensation system. To be effective, it should have several desirable characteristics:

1. "The system must fit appropriately with the mission statement of the institution" (Diamond, 1993b, pp. 18–19). A strong connection or link should exist among institutional goals, improved faculty performance, additional compensation, and acceptance of increased compensation as an incentive (Lauer, 1991, p. 52). Higher education's current environment suggests that every institution wishing to survive and grow should carefully assess its faculty compensation system and ensure alignment with the institution's mission. For this alignment to occur, it may be necessary to rewrite the institution's mission statement, making it "realistic, operational, and sensitive to the unique characteristics and strengths of the institution" (Diamond, 1993b, p. 8).

2. "The system must be sensitive to the differences among the disciplines" (Diamond, 1993b, p. 19). Standards of appropriate faculty activity vary from one discipline to another. For some, basic research has the greatest value, while for others, public service or undergraduate teaching may be relatively more important. Several authors encourage higher education faculty to adopt a broader definition of scholarship and to broaden the activities for which a faculty member can receive reward (see Boyer, 1990 Rice, 1991).

3. "The system must be sensitive to differences among individuals" (Diamond, 1993b, p. 19). Sometimes, higher education institutions hold every faculty member to the same standard and do not take advantage of particular strengths of individual faculty members. Establishing a common standard for evaluating all faculty members, however, "is unrealistic and can undermine the quality of an academic unit. The truth is that outstanding researchers are not necessarily great teachers, and great teachers are not always experienced researchers" (Diamond, 1993b, p. 9).

Rather than force every individual into the same form, "the goal for each department, school, or college should be to bring together talented individuals who can work together in a synergistic manner to reach the unit's goals" (Diamond, 1993b, p. 9).

4. "The system must be sensitive to standards established by regional, state, and disciplinary accreditation associations" (Diamond, 1993b, p. 10).

5. "The system must develop and incorporate an assessment program that is appropriate, perceived to be fair, and workable" (Diamond, 1993b, p. 21).

Safeguards need to be built into any compensation system to ensure that decisions are based on objective performance criteria and not personal judgment.

Although these five characteristics of an effective compensation system are desirable, an institution deciding a change knows that "the devil is in the details." As a consequence, an institution may be forced by conflicts among stakeholders (faculty, administration, governing board, state priorities, and state and regional leaders) to be unable to develop a compensation system that achieves all these strengths. Trade-offs are inevitable between what is desirable and what can actually be achieved. The next section describes how one institution redesigned its faculty compensation system using many of the suggestions listed above.

Trade-offs are inevitable between what is desirable and what can actually be achieved.

One Institution's Redesign of Its Faculty Compensation System

In the early 1990s, the University of Maryland system "required that each institution revise its mission statement, with the aim of making statements more specific and more complementary" (McMahon and Caret, 1997, p. 13). Towson State University (TSU), now Towson University, was one of the institutions affected that had earlier determined, on its own, that many of its faculty "as individuals focused on their own needs rather than those of the student or the institution" (p. 15). After reconstructing the university's mission statement, the institution began a process of changing the faculty roles and rewards structure. A number of forums on campus were conducted over two years, and an ad hoc promotion and tenure committee from the faculty senate as well as a university task force on faculty roles and rewards simultaneously began discussing how to improve the faculty compensation system (pp. 16–17). The final result was a system that "(1) . . . allowed for flexible and varying faculty profiles, all leading to successful career paths at the institution, (2) . . . suggested a workload profile for each academic year, (3) . . . broadened . . . views on scholarship, (4) [had department chairs serve as coordinators to ensure that the faculty of each department jointly produced the necessary variety of output], (5) . . . [recommended] faculty review . . . over a broad period of time, say three to five years, to provide the 'complete' faculty member that TSU needed" (pp. 17–18).

The final merit faculty compensation system that emerged at TSU has the following characteristics: "[It] gave guidance and direction to the faculty; . . . was simple, flexible, and adaptable; . . . allowed for variance from evaluation period to evaluation period such that no label is attached to the faculty member on a permanent basis, . . . [faculty were alternatively evaluated under a different profile that] was most appropriate for the period of evaluation; . . . philosophically fit the campus culture; . . . sustained the continuous growth and development of the faculty; reflected collaboration and cooperation among individuals; . . . valued differences" (McMahon and Caret, 1997, pp. 19–20). Because of the central role of department chairs as coordinators and guides to faculty, chairs at TSU had to be retrained because "normalizing the chairs' efforts to a reasonable degree across campus is also vital" (p. 20).

Several new initiatives grew out of the redesign of TSU's faculty compensation system: (1) a guidebook to the faculty role and reward process at TSU to explain to faculty the institution's mission and how the faculty workload affects the day-to-day activity of faculty members, (2) a university teaching initiative, which evolved into the Center for Instructional Advancement and Technology started to aid in faculty development, (3) a merit pay program developed by the faculty governing body to support the institution's change in the faculty roles and reward structure, (4) development by every individual department of its own criteria under the new merit pay program guidelines as determined by the university senate (McMahon and Caret, 1997, pp. 20–21).

The process of change at TSU took seven years but represents an example of how a complex institution can bring about fundamental changes in the behavior of its faculty. The institution, at the time the report was published, had been able to change its overall direction from a chaotic one with individual faculty writing their own agendas to one where the faculty jointly but individually worked to support the institution's mission.

Other reports of institutional changes to redirect faculty behavior include Abdelal, Blumenfeld, Crimmins, and Dressel (1997) and Schallenkamp, Davis, and Lee (1997). Houpt and others (1997, p. 185) described change in direction at a medical school.

Constructing an Effective Faculty Merit Compensation System

Some of the implications that make for a successful merit compensation system listed previously in Table 3 may be difficult for an institution of higher education to implement and achieve. Some are particularly relevant for higher education, and others are less so. Because of this mixture of positive and negative implications, "there [is] probably no other activity that has more potential for strengthening or weakening the [academic] department" (Gilchrist and White, 1990, p. 249). Moreover, "few issues in higher education spark as much anger and anxiety as the mention of merit pay salary adjustments" (Crawford, Hirsch, and Valentine, 1984, p. 18).

For a merit faculty compensation system to be successful at any higher education institution, it has been suggested that the five structural conditions summarized in Table 5 be present (Griffith and Neugarten, 1984, pp. 74–79). Moreover, some important questions must be answered in the adoption of a merit compensation system (see Table 6).

TABLE 5
Structural Conditions for a Successful Merit System at an Institution of Higher Education

1. Faculty must believe that effective performance directly causes higher compensation.

2. Faculty have some control over the criteria used to measure their performance.

3. High-performing faculty are able to earn compensation significantly higher than the base earned by colleagues with lower performance levels.

4. Compensation at an institution with a merit system should not be affected by factors beyond the control of individual faculty.

5. There must be ways to minimize negative consequences of earning larger merit increases than others on the faculty.

Source: Griffith & Neugarten, 1984, pp. 74–79.

Tables 5 and 6 present the issues that face an institution of higher education from different viewpoints. Who actually establishes the parameters of the merit system represents an important notable entry in both tables. In a discussion of the problems with merit systems cited in the literature, an important common criticism is that faculty claim merit systems are set up and used by the administration to manipulate and control faculty behavior. This situation would be more probable at institutions where the merit system is established with little faculty input. It would be less likely at those institutions where the faculty established the parameters of the system. If an institution implements a merit faculty compensation system in place of a preexisting single salary system, the signals communicated to the faculty and the culture of the institution change from one of "a welfare system, where all people received the same pay increase, to a competitive business where pay increases are contingent on performance . . . because it signifies a prevailing organizational belief that work is to be rewarded on the basis of performance rather than on the basis of equality, need, or seniority" (Heneman, 1992, p. 9).

TABLE 6
Questions to Be Answered in Adopting a Merit Compensation System at an Institution of Higher Education

1. What constitutes good faculty performance?

2. What are specific standards for outstanding, acceptable, and insufficient faculty performance?

3. How can the specific standards be measured?

4. How can standards be made comparable for different disciplines?

5. Who develops performance standards, faculty or administrators?

6. With scarce financial resources, how can meaningful above-base merit awards be realized?

7. How can faculty significantly influence their own compensation when funding increases are determined largely by external forces?

8. How can individual objectives be balanced with institutional objectives to avoid divisive competitiveness among faculty?

Constructing a Single Salary System

If an institution determines a single salary system is best for its campus, it must try to minimize the decreases in optimal allocation of faculty by some means. The following discussion focuses on four suggestions (Beaumont, 1978, p. 20) to improve the human resource allocation characteristics of a single salary schedule.

- *Frequent changes in the single salary schedule to keep salaries close to the (estimated) equilibrium real wage.* Many faculty consider a single salary schedule with annual percentage increases large enough to maintain faculty purchasing power over time to be equitable because individuals would not have to worry about maintaining a consistent level of real income. In other words, faculty believe "that they should share in economy-wide productivity gains [which increase personal income in general]" (Hansen, 1988, p. 11). If the single salary schedule keeps pace with inflation, high quality faculty with a career objective of being a professor will not be given an incentive to shun higher education.

- *Adjustments in the single salary schedule initial appointments at higher ranks and/or accelerated promotions.* A campus interested in obtaining high quality faculty to work within a single salary schedule may be forced to hire them at fairly high initial compensation levels and accelerate their movement through the system's cells. Salary compression and perhaps lower morale among average faculty may be the problems that follow such a policy.

- *Changes in the nonpecuniary circumstances of employment.* Providing faculty with smaller teaching loads, quality offices, well stocked laboratories, and the latest advances in instructional and office technology are fringe benefits that perhaps can make up for problems resulting from a single salary schedule.

- *Quality adjustments, as when a single salary schedule wage that is "too low" prevents departments from obtaining the desired number of highest quality faculty.* Instead of granting nonpecuniary benefits to all faculty, only "highest quality" faculty would be given an incentive to become a faculty member at a single salary schedule institution or encouraged to remain.

Conclusions and Recommendations

HIGHER EDUCATION DECISION MAKERS are focusing their attention on management practices and procedures to respond to the growing demands for academic quality and accountability from a variety of sources. Strategic planning and mission statements are widely accepted tools employed by institutions to respond to these demands. This report encourages the use of another management tool, faculty compensation. The discussion began with two conceptual premises: the absolute and relative levels of faculty compensation do have an impact on faculty behavior, and faculty behavior and its relation to the employing institution's mission can be positive, negative, or neutral depending on the specific details of the compensation system in use. The first premise challenges the conventional wisdom about individual faculty attitudes with respect to compensation. It long has been assumed, or perhaps idealized, that faculty care little for financial extrinsic reward but are more concerned with implicit rewards, such as living the intellectual life and educating students. A casual review of the scholarly literature on faculty compensation, however, convinces a reader that the conventional wisdom may be incorrect and probably unrealistic.

The first conceptual premise implies that faculty compensation affects faculty activities, performance, satisfaction, morale, and the signals faculty perceive with respect to the institution's expectations about faculty behavior. If faculty perceive contradictory or unclear signals about what their behavior should be, they may pursue their own goals and objectives rather than the institution's. Faculty behavior should be primarily a function of the institution's mission statement rather than something determined by individual faculty considering themselves independent contractors hired by the institution. Thus, faculty activity will produce the most public good when governed by the institution's mission, not by administrative fiat or individual faculty members.

The second conceptual premise implies that faculty compensation can be a management tool the institution can use to translate financial resources into rewards to alter faculty performance. The compensation system thus becomes a link between financial resources and faculty behavior to achieve the institution's goals. Institutions that align faculty behavior with the institutional mission will be more successful in avoiding public criticism, improving the public's perception of the quality of the institution, and, as a result, securing increased funding. As pressure mounts for accountability, from both inside and outside the institution, faculty compensation can be an effective policy to align faculty behavior with institutional mission. Further, this arrangement can likely improve the institution's success in meeting expectations for accountability. Any lack of congruity between mission and the faculty reward structure should be addressed and resolved. This is one of the challenges for higher education in the twenty-first century.

The review of the literature on faculty compensation suggests several conclusions:

1. Both traditional merit and single salary systems of faculty compensation have advantages and disadvantages.
2. No one type of faculty compensation system is an ideal for all institutions to adopt. In fact, each institution has to carefully examine the various types of compensation systems, taking into account its own culture, history, political realities, and faculty to determine the best compensation system for it.
3. An institution that decides to change its faculty compensation system should follow the guidelines outlined in the section on designing a compensation system.

A merit compensation system for higher education faculty represents a plan that has great implicit appeal. Its biggest institutional advantage lies in its political and cultural acceptability, making it consistent with the basic cultural norms of the United States that link compensation to performance. The advantage of a faculty merit compensation system represents a powerful and undeniable benefit for an institution. Once in place, however, operational disadvantages may appear.

The operational disadvantages of a faculty merit compensation system range from difficulty in establishing an equitable or fair system to excessive paperwork needed to comply with reporting requirements, to less collegiality, collaboration, and cohesiveness among faculty. In addition, merit systems increase opportunities for subjective compensation decision making by administrators. Additional concerns include a reduction in the relative importance of teaching effectiveness, a reduction in service activity by faculty, and a reduction in scholarship quality while increasing quantity.

A single salary schedule has the advantages of being easy to administer, generally accepted by faculty as fair and equitable, and promoting collegiality and cooperation among faculty. Faculty report that a single salary schedule provides good faculty morale, more meaningful scholarship, and an emphasis on effective teaching. As for disadvantages, a single salary schedule rewards faculty tenure more than performance: it bases an individual's compensation on historical data, which makes it somewhat culturally unacceptable and opens the institution to public censure.

Even though no one faculty compensation system is the best one for all types of institutions, the following suggestions are implied in the literature.

1. Research institutions have long used a merit compensation system for their faculty without severe problems. Consequently, a pure faculty merit compensation system appears to be appropriate to a research institution. The only caveat would be that the institution avoid the operational disadvantages discussed above as much as possible.

2. For nonresearch-oriented institutions with a stated primary mission of undergraduate teaching and professional service but no stated mission emphasis on scholarship, a combination of a single salary and a merit

system would be most appropriate. The authors of this report prefer the elements found in the California step system (Manaster, 1985).

3. For nonresearch-oriented institutions with only undergraduate teaching for its stated mission (two-year institutions and small liberal arts institutions), a single salary schedule would be the most appropriate system, provided there are ways to appropriately deal with faculty who are not working to support the institutional mission.

Institutions should follow the various guidelines and steps discussed in the section dealing with designing an effective system. These guidelines and steps should help an institution develop a compensation system that is aligned with its institutional mission, generally accepted by faculty and administrators, and easily understood by faculty who can use the system to determine their own behavior. Towson State University's experience represents a good application of these guidelines and steps, and an institution that follows the TSU model should be successful in creating a worthwhile faculty compensation system.

Appendix A: Illustrative Criteria for Faculty Merit Awards

Teaching

Mandatory Criteria:

1. Consistently well organized

2. Consistently well prepared
   - Demonstrates consistent and comprehensive knowledge of subject material
   - Keeps content updated: uses research, updates bibliography

3. Consistently displays enthusiasm and interest in class preparation

4. Encourages opinions and relevant disagreement from students

5. Maintains a climate of fair and impartial interaction with students

6. Demonstrates excellent verbal communication techniques to enhance classroom learning

7. Demonstrates ability to relate theory to practice

Meets at Least Two of the Following Criteria:

1. Develops and maintains creative learning materials to enhance classroom learning
   - For self-use
   - For department

2. Develops or collaboratively develops an elective course that is approved for teaching

---

3. Contributes to curriculum planning group
   - Chair of curriculum planning group
   - Develops or assists in developing new or revised courses

4. Develops and uses evaluation procedures based on course objectives
   - Tests and/or written assignments
   - Clinical evaluation tools

5. Seeks improvement in both teaching and evaluation methods, for example
   - Attends workshops, in-service programs, continuing education courses
   - Takes courses related to professional growth

6. Participates in or directs an honors fellowship grant, thesis/dissertation, or honors project

The applicant must document meeting these criteria through the use of peer evaluations, student evaluations, administrative evaluations, or other specific materials that directly demonstrate excellence in teaching.

Scholarly Productivity
Qualifies for Merit Salary Supplement by Meeting One of the Following Criteria:

1. Engages in research project and/or writes or participates in writing report(s) of the results

2. Has manuscript accepted for publication

3. Authors instructional materials including but not limited to:
   - Textbook
   - Audiovisual programs
   - Computer software

4. Serves as reviewer for publisher

5. Serves as a member of editorial board for professional publications

6. Writes grants
   - Submits proposals
   - Awarded grant

7. Makes presentation at professional meeting

Service

Mandatory Criteria:

1. Attends international, national, regional, and/or state professional meetings
   - Represents university, college, or department
   - Attends for own enhancement at own expense

2. Attends local professional meetings regularly

3. Serves professional organizations in one of four capacities:
   - Officer
   - Committee member
   - Delegate to meetings
   - Attends meeting at own expense and reports back

4. Participates in community activities

Serves in Two of Six Areas:

1. Serves as a regular consultant to community agencies

2. Serves as an active board member of a recognized community group
   - Active member
   - Officer
   - Committee chair

3. Serves on university committees
   - Active member
   - Officer

4. Assists in developing courses outside the university (for public or private schools, community organizations, public service groups, for example)
   - Consultation service
   - Cooperative teaching with other departments
   - Assists in developing interdisciplinary course in university

5. Actively recruits nursing students for Ball State University

6. Item writer for standardized test.

Source: Elliott & Ryan, 1986, p. 132.

Appendix B: Evaluation Tool for Satisfactory Faculty Standards

Criteria	Yes	No	N/A

Instruction

1. Assists with planning for and teaches the content identified
   - Identifies the needs of the student as a person, citizen, and professional nurse in planning course content
   - Considers the educational objectives of the program
   - Plans the learning experiences of students within the department, nursing facilities, and services

2. Helps maintain a current file of all materials used in instruction

3. Teaches and assists with teaching of other courses and related responsibilities as delegated

Departmental

1. Assists in evaluating and implementing the nursing education program as it relates to the department's philosophy and objectives and in conjunction with the trends and developmental needs of the profession

2. Participates in departmental committee meetings

Criteria	Yes	No	N/A

Guidance

1. Provides academic and course-related guidance as appropriate

Research

1. Assists with the planning and development of organized research inquiry into problems, the department, and/or the clinical area

   - Identifies problem areas for investigation and study
   - Provides data applicable to a study or investigation being conducted

University

1. Complies with college and university policies and regulations

Summary

1. Meets criteria as outlined in departmental job description

Source: Elliott & Ryan, 1986, p. 130.

References

Abdelal, A. T., Blumenfeld, D. C., Crimmins, T. J., and Dressel, P. L. (1997). Integrating accountability systems and reward structures: Workload policy, post-tenure evaluations, and salary compensation. *Metropolitan Universities, 7*(4), 61–73.

American Association of University Professors, Committee on College and University Teaching, Research, and Publication. (1996). The politics of intervention: External regulation of academic activities and workloads in public higher education. *Academe, 82*(1), 46–52.

Aristotle. 1998. *The Nicomachean Ethics.* D. Ross, translator. New York: Oxford University Press.

Barber, L. W., and Klein, K. (1983). Merit pay and teacher evaluation. *Phi Delta Kappan, 65*(4), 247–251.

Barnett, H., Cohen, J. L., Jeffries, P., and Rosen, W. (1988). Coping with merit pay. *Academe, 74*(6), 19–22.

Bassett, G. (1994). Merit pay increases are a mistake. *Compensation and Benefits Review, 26*(2), 20–21.

Beaumont, M. S. (1978). Efficiency and equity: The single salary schedule in public higher education. *AAUP Bulletin, 64*(1), 19–25.

Beaumont, M. S. (1985). *Salary systems in public higher education.* New York: Praeger.

Bell, L. A. (1998). Doing better: The annual report on the economic status of the profession 1997–98. *Academe, 84*(2), 15–21.

Bell, L. A. (2000). More good news, so why the blues? The annual report on the economic status of the profession, 1999–2000. *Academe, 86*(2), 12–37.

Benjamin, R. (1998). Looming deficits: Causes, consequences, and cures. *Change, 30*(2), 12–17.

Bok, D. (1992). Reclaiming the public trust. *Change, 24*(4), 13–19.

Bowen, H. (1968). Faculty salaries: Past and present. *Educational Record, 49*(1), 9–21.

Bowen, H. (1978). *Academic compensation: Are faculty and staff in American higher education adequately paid?* New York: Teachers Insurance and Annuity Association/College Retirement Equities Fund.

Bowers, R. G., and Breuder, R. L. (1982). A faculty salary system that works. *Community and Junior College Journal, 52*(8), 32–35.

Boyer, E. L. (1990). *Scholarship Reconsidered: Priorities of the Professoriate*. San Francisco: Jossey-Bass.

Breslin, R. D., and Klagholz, L. F. (1980). Paying faculty members what they are worth. *Educational Record, 61*(1), 43–44.

Brewer, P. D., Brewer, V. L, and Hilton, C. (1990). Promoting research productivity in colleges of business. *Journal of Education for Business, 66*(1), 52–56.

Burke, J. C., and Serban, A. M. (1998). Performance funding: Fashionable fad or emerging trend? *Community College Journal, 63*(3), 26–29.

Burke, R. R. (1988). *Research on the effects of rewards: Implications for annual merit pay*. Presentation at the annual meeting of the Association of Teacher Educators. (ED 294 854)

Calhoun, F. S. (1983). *Merit pay plans for teachers: Status and descriptions*. Arlington, VA: Educational Research Service.

Chaffee, E. E., and Sherr, L. A. (1992). *Quality: Transforming postsecondary education*. ASHE-ERIC Higher Education Report, no. 3. Washington, DC: Graduate School of Education and Human Development, The George Washington University.

Chait, R. (1988). Providing group rewards for group performance. *Academe, 74*(6), 23–24.

Clardy, A. (1988). *Compensation systems and school effectiveness: Merit pay as an incentive for school improvement*. Position Paper. (ED 335 789)

Clevenger, T., Jr. (1989, October). An algorithmic system for determining faculty salaries. *ACA Bulletin, 70*, 8–13.

Cornesky, R., McCool, S., Byrnes, L., and Weber, R. (1992). *Implementing Total Quality Management in Higher Education*. Madison, Wis.: Magna Publications, Inc.

Counelis, J. S. (1984, November). *Merit compensation and higher education*. Paper presented at the annual meeting of the American Educational Studies Association. (ED 252 124)

Crawford, J. E., Hirsch, R. O., and Valentine, C. A. (1984, August). Top third/bottom third: A humane approach to merit pay for academic departments. *Association for Communication Administration Bulletin, 49*, 18–20.

Dennis, L. J. (1982). "Why not merit pay? *Contemporary Education, 54*(1), 18–21.

Diamond, R. M. (1993a). Changing priorities and the faculty reward system. In R. M. Diamond and B. E. Adam (Eds.), *Recognizing faculty work: Reward systems for the year 2000* (pp. 5–12). New Directions for Higher Education, no. 81. San Francisco: Jossey-Bass.

Diamond, R. M. (1993b). How to change the faculty reward system. *Trusteeship, 1*(5), 17–21.

Diamond, R. M. (1999). *Aligning faculty rewards with institutional mission: Statements, policies, and guidelines*. Bolton, Mass.: Anker.

Economic Report of the President 1997. Washington, D.C.: United States Government Printing Office.

Elliott, S. M., and Ryan, M. E. (1986). A market and merit plan for faculty salary increases. *College Teaching, 34*(4), 129–134.

Evans, W. A. (1970). Pay for performance: Fact of fable. *Personnel Journal, 726*–731.

Eymonerie, M. (1980). Salary scales: pros and cons. *Academe, 66*(2), 118–119.

Fairweather, J. S. (1993a). Academic values and faculty rewards. *Review of Higher Education, 17*(1), 43–68.

Fairweather, J. S. (1993b). Faculty reward structures: Toward institutional and professional homogenization. *Research in Higher Education, 34*(5), 603–623.

Fairweather, J. S. (1995). Myths and realities of academic labor markets. *Economics of Education Review, 14*(2), 179–192.

Fassiotto, M. E. (1986). *The merit of merit: Notes on the arguments for and against merit systems.* Position Paper. (ED 271 040)

Florestano, P. S., and Hambrick, R. (1984). Rewarding faculty for profession-related public service. *Educational Record, 65*(1), 18–21.

Foldesi, R. S. (1996). Higher education compensation systems of the future. *CUPA Journal, 47*(2), 29–32.

Fox, C. J., and Cochran, C. E. (1990). Discretion advocacy in public administration theory. *Administration & Society, 22*(2), 249–272.

Freed, J. E., Klugman, M. R., and Fife, J. D. (1997). *A culture for academic excellence: Implementing the quality principles in higher education.* ASHE-ERIC Higher Education Report, vol. 25, no. 1. Washington, DC: Graduate School of Education and Human Development, The George Washington University.

Gilchrist, J. A., and White, K. D. (1990). Policy development and satisfaction with merit pay: A field study in a university setting. *College Student Journal, 24*(3), 249–254.

Green, D. (Ed.). (1994). *What is quality in higher education?* Bristol, Penn.: Taylor & Francis.

Griffith, W. I., and Neugarten, D. A. (1984). Rewarding teacher excellence: Organizational issues and obstacles. *Teaching Sociology, 12*(1), 71–81.

Guzzo, R. A., Jette, R. D., and Katzell, R. A. (1985). The effects of psychologically based intervention programs on worker productivity: A meta-analysis. *Personnel Psychology, 38*(2), 75–291.

Hammond, C. M. J., and McDermott, J. C. (1997). Merit-based pay won't motivate faculty. *Thought & Action: The NEA Higher Education Journal, 13*(2), 107–112.

Hansen, W. L. (1979). *Academic compensation: Myths and realities.* Paper presented at the annual Academic Planning Conference. (ED 181 822)

Hansen, W. L. (1988). Merit pay in structured and unstructured salary systems. *Academe, 74*(6), 10–13.

Healy, P., and Hebel, S. (1999, June 11). Debate over CUNY's future intensifies. *Chronicle of Higher Education, 45*(40), A34.

Hearn, J. C. (1999). Pay and performance in the university: An examination of faculty salaries. *Review of Higher Education, 22*(4), 391–410.

Heneman, R. L. (1992). *Merit pay: Linking pay increases to performance ratings.* Reading, Mass.: Addison-Wesley.

Hooker, C. P. (1978). A behavior modification model for Merit U. *Phi Delta Kappan, 59*(7), 48.

Hopkins, B. L. (1992). *Pay for performance: History, Controversy, and Evidence.* New York: The Haworth Press. Inc.

Houpt, J. L., and others. (1997). How medical schools can maintain quality while adapting to resource constraints. *Academic Medicine, 72*(3), 180–185.

Hunnicutt, G. G., Taylor, R. L., and Keeffe, M. J. (1991). An exploratory examination of faculty evaluation and merit compensation systems in Texas colleges and universities. *CUPA Journal, 42*(1), 13–21.

Johnson, S. M. (1984a). Merit pay for teachers: A poor prescription for reform. *Harvard Educational Review, 54*(2), 175–185.

Johnson, S. M. (1984b). *Pros and cons of merit pay.* Bloomington, Ind.: Phi Delta Kappa Educational Foundation.

Kasten, K. L. (1984). Tenure and merit pay as rewards for research, teaching, and service at a research university. *Journal of Higher Education, 55*(4), 500–514.

Keane, J. A. (1978). *Characteristics of merit rating based salary plans at a number of small private American colleges.* Position Paper. (ED 153 554)

Kitsuse, A. (1992). Down with merit-pay increases. *Across the Board, 29*(2), 23–27.

Kohn, A. (1993a). *Punished by rewards: The trouble with gold stars, incentive plans, A's, praise, and other bribes.* New York: Houghton Mifflin.

Kohn, A. (1993b). Why incentive plans cannot work. *Harvard Business Review, 71*(5), 54–63.

Konrad, A. M., and Pfeffer, J. (1990). Do you get what you deserve? Factors affecting the relationship between productivity and pay. *Administrative Science Quarterly, 35*(2), 258–285.

Lauer, L. A. (1991). Searching for answers: Should universities create merit pay systems? *NACUBO Business Officer, 25*(5), 52–54.

Layzell, D. T. (1996). Faculty workload and productivity: Recurrent issues with new imperatives. *Review of Higher Education, 19*(3), 267–281.

Lenington, R. L. (1996). *Managing higher education as a business.* Phoenix, Ariz.: Oryx Press.

Lewis, L. S. (1996). *Marginal worth: Teaching and the Academic Labor Market.* New Brunswick, NJ: Transaction Publishers.

Lillydahl, J. H., and Singell, L. D. (1993). Job satisfaction, salaries and unions: The determination of university faculty compensation. *Economics of Education Review, 12*(3), 234–243.

MacKay, J. H. (1985). Market, merit, and experience at Oakland University. *Academe, 71*(4), 17–22.

Magnusen, K. O. (1987). Faculty evaluation, performance, and pay: Application and issues. *Journal of Higher Education, 58*(5), 516–529.

Manaster, A. (1985). The California "step system." *Academe, 71*(4), 23–26.

Mangan, K. S. (1996, July 26). Medical schools are reining in the salaries of faculty members. *Chronicle of Higher Education, 42*(46), A16.

Marchant, G. J., and Newman, I. (1994). Faculty activities and rewards: Views from education administrators in the USA. *Assessment & Evaluation in Higher Education, 19*(2), 145–152.

McKay, J. R. (1986, April). *Merit pay: A plan that works.* Paper presented at the National Conference on Faculty Evaluation and Development. (ED 270 181)

McMahon, J. D., and Caret, R. L. (1997). Redesigning the faculty roles and rewards structure. *Metropolitan Universities, 7*(4), 11–22.

Mickler, M. L. (1987). Merit pay: Boon or boondoggle? *The Clearing House, 61*(3), 137–141.

Miller, K. T. (1992). Merit pay from the faculty's perspective. *CUPA Journal, 43*(3), 7–16.

Missouri Coordinating Board for Higher Education. (1998). *Blueprint for Missouri higher education: 1998 report on progress toward the statewide public policy initiatives and goals for Missouri higher education.* (ED 421 048)

Mooney, C. J. (1991). Efforts to cut amount of "trivial" scholarship win new backing from many academics. *Chronicle of Higher Education, 37*(36), A1–A13.

Murnane, R. J., and Cohen, D. K. (1986). Merit pay and the evaluation problem: Why most merit pay plans fail and a few survive. *Harvard Educational Review, 56*(1), 1–17.

Neumann, Y., and Finaly-Neumann, E. (1990). The reward-support framework and faculty commitment to their university. *Research in Higher Education, 31*(1), 75–97.

Osif, B. A., and Harwood, R. L. (1995). Employee compensation. *Library Administration & Management, 9*(4), 241–245.

Pratt, L. R. (1988). Merit pay: Reaganomics for the faculty? *Academe, 74*(6), 14–16.

Prewit, L. B., Phillips, J. D., and Yasin, K. (1991). Merit pay in academia: Perceptions from the School of Business. *Public Personnel Management, 20*(4), 409–417.

Renner, R. R., and Jester, R. E. (1980). Fair salaries and faculty effort: Is there a connection? *Southern Journal of Educational Research, 14*(2), 159–169.

Rice, R. E. (1991). "The New American Scholar: Scholarship and the purposes of the university." *Metropolitan Universities Journal, 1*(4), 7–18.

Schallenkamp, K. K., Davis, L. W., and Lee, R. C. (1997). Mission, values, and effecting change: A case study. *Metropolitan Universities, 7*(4), 31–42.

Schmidt, P. (1999, July 2). A state transforms colleges with "performance funding." *Chronicle of Higher Education, 45*(43), A26–A28.

Selingo, J. (1999, June 11). New chancellor shakes up Cal. State with ambitious agenda and blunt style. *Chronicle of Higher Education, 45*(40), A32–A34.

Shreeve, W., and others. (1985). Contracting for merit pay. *College Teaching, 33*(4), 155–158.

Smith, A. (1976). *An inquiry into the nature and causes of the wealth of nations.* Chicago: University of Chicago Press.

Taylor, R. L., Hunnicutt, G. G., and Keeffe, M. J. (1991). Merit pay in academia: Historical perspectives and contemporary perceptions. *Review of Public Administration, 11*(3), 51–65.

Tharp, J. (1991). When merit pay fails: Searching for an alternative. *NASPA Journal, 29*(1), 75–79.

Tuckman, B. H., and Tuckman, H. P. (1976). The structure of salaries at American Universities. *Journal of Higher Education, 47*(1), 51–64.

Van Fleet, D. D. (1972). Salary administration in higher education: A tentative plan. *AAUP Bulletin, 58*(4), 413–418.

Wergin, J. F., and Swingen, J. N. (1999). *Evaluation of academic departments: A strategy for the Pew Charitable Trusts.* Report prepared for the Pew Colloquium on Quality Assurance in Academic Departments.

Winston, G. C. (1998). The dismal science of higher education. *Trusteeship, 6*(4), 16–19.

Wood, P. H., and Burke, R. R. (1989). *College faculty attitudes toward merit pay.* Research Report. (ED 319 290)

Wood, P. H., and Wood, J. H. (1988, February 17). *Annual merit pay and the evaluation and improvement of college faculty: Problems, solutions, and more problems.* Presentation at the annual meeting of the Association of Teacher Educators. (ED 309 696)

Name Index

A

Abdelal, A. T., 18, 63
American Association of University
   Professors, 2
Aristotle, 50

B

Barnett, H., 34
Bassett, G., 44
Beaumont, M. S., 15, 17, 32, 47, 49, 65
Bell, L. A., 11, 12, 14
Benjamin, R., 5, 6
Blumenfeld, D. C., 18, 63
Bok, D., iii, 1
Bowen, H., 11, 12, 13, 14
Bowers, R. G., 21
Boyer, E. L., 60
Breslin, R. D., 7
Breuder, R. L., 21
Brewer, P. D., 34, 40
Brewer, V. L., 34, 40
Burke, J. C., iii
Burke, R. R., 38, 40, 41
Byrnes, L., 9

C

Calhoun, F. S., 35, 38
Caret, R. L., 1, 2, 61, 62, 63
Chaffee, E. E., 9
Chait, R., 23, 43, 53
Clardy, A., 35, 49, 57
Clevenger, T., Jr., 22, 23, 52

Cochran, C. E., 36
Cohen, D. K., 55
Cohen, J. L., 34
Cornesky, R., 9
Counelis, J. S., 43
Crawford, J. E., 63
Crimmins, T. J., 18, 63

D

Davis, L. W., 63
Dennis, L. J., 37, 42
Diamond, R. M., 5, 9, 55, 60, 61
Dressel, P. L., 18, 63

E

Economic Report of the President, 14
Elliott, S. M., 16, 19, 42, 43, 44, 46,
   73, 76
Evans, W. A., 26
Eymonerie, M., 19

F

Fairweather, J. S., 8, 34
Fassiotto, M. E., 33, 35, 36, 38
Fife, J. D., 57
Finaly-Neumann, E., 56
Florestano, P. S., 23, 41
Foldesi, R. S., 7, 47, 49
Fox, C. J., 36
Freed, J. E., 57

Shreeve, W., 21, 51
Singell, L. D., 5, 12, 13
Smith, A., 26
Swingen, J. N., 23

T

Taylor, R. L., 6, 8, 36, 37, 38, 40, 41, 42
Tharp, J., 17, 18, 37, 50
Tuckman, B. H., 8, 9
Tuckman, H. P., 8, 9

V

Valentine, C. A., 63
Van Fleet, D. D., 22, 52

W

Weber, R., 9
Wergin, J. F., 23
White, K. D., 38, 41, 63
Winston, G. C., iii, 1
Wood, J. H., 41
Wood, P. H., 38, 40, 41

Y

Yasin, K., 8

Subject Index

A

Accountability: CUNY program, 2; demands for quality and, 67; faculty compensation and, vii

Adjustments: compensation, 66; for unjustified distortions, 22–23, 52

Advantages: in higher education, 14; merit compensation systems, 33–36, 69; nontraditional systems, 50–53; single salary systems, 47–49, 69. *See also* Disadvantages; Operational advantages; Operational disadvantages

Aristotelian view, 32

B

Behaviorism, 27

C

Challenges: designing effective systems, 55; facing institutions of higher education, iii–iv

City University of New York (CUNY) debate over future, 2

Clark, John Bates, 26–27, 30

Combination systems: Ball State University, 16, 19; Eastern Washington University, 21–22, 51; Oakland University, 19–20; University of California, 20; Williamsport Area Community College, 21

Compensation systems. *See* Faculty compensation systems

Contract merit systems. *See* Merit compensation systems

Cost of living adjustments. *See* Adjustments

CPI compared to RFC, 11–12

Criteria: for faculty merit awards, 71–72; need for objective, 61

D

Design considerations: challenges, 55; constructing effective systems, 63–65; faculty compensation system examples, 61–63; recommendations, 9, 67–70; steps to follow, 56–61

Disadvantages: merit compensation systems, 37–46, 69; single salary systems, 49–50. *See also* Advantages; Operational advantages; Operational disadvantages

Distortion, adjustments for unjustified, 22–23, 52

E

Economic growth and faculty compensation, 11–14

Economic man concept, 26

Economic theories supporting merit pay: efficiency wage theory, 31; implicit contract theory, 30–31; marginal productivity theory, 26–27, 30

Employment opportunities, alternatives, 13

Evaluation considerations: ambiguity in process, 39; for existing compensation system, 57–58; forms for faculty productivity, 19, 75–76; process, 40, 42

F

Faculty: and administration, 43–44, 64; behavior of, 67–68; evaluation impact on relationships, 39, 41; non-tenured, 46; team rewards, 23, 52–53; workloads examined, 2

Faculty compensation: adjusting for unjustified distortions, 22–23, 52; historical perspective, 11–14; internal factors determining, 7–9; issues affecting, iv, 6–7; linked to funds generated, 23–24, 53

Faculty compensation systems: addressing nine subthemes, 4; characteristics of ideal, 9, 58–60; contract salary systems, 15, 16; factors affecting, vii–viii; need for understanding, 3. *See also* Merit compensation systems; Nontraditional faculty compensation systems; Single salary schedule (systems)

Faculty self-development review, 17–18, 50

Feedback mechanism, 7

Funding: control over, 6–7; ramifications of insufficient, 45

Funds, requirement for faculty to generate, 23–24, 53

H

Higher education: compensation systems identified, 15; historical perspective for compensation, 11–14; rewarding service, 23; roles as agent, 7

I

Incentive pay. *See* Merit pay

Incentives: South Carolina plan, 2–3; using faculty self-development reviews, 18

Income. *See* Faculty compensation

Industrial Revolution and compensation, 26

Inflation, compensation systems and, 65–66

Initiatives example, 61–63

Institutional quality. *See* Quality

Inversion, 13

Issues: addressing faculty compensation, iv; facing higher education, 1–4

M

Market pay concept, 13

Matrix. *See* Step systems

Measurements: delineating factors, 37; time required to create, 42

Merit compensation systems: advantages and disadvantages, 33–36, 37–46, 69; constructing effective, 63–65; contract merit systems, 21–22, 51; salary administration with, 22–24, 51–52; single salary combined with, 50–51. *See also* Faculty compensation systems

Merit evaluation form, 16

Merit pay: economic theories supporting, 26–27, 30–31; psychological theories supporting, 27–30

Mission statements: as guides for designing system, 57; importance of achieving, 5; system must fit with, 60

Motivators: merit increases as, 34–35; middle group, 43; self-satisfaction as, 44. *See also* Incentives

N

Nontraditional faculty compensation systems: contract merit systems, 21–22; defined, 15; faculty self-development review, 17–18; operational advantages, 50–53; salary administration with merit compensation, 22–24; single salary combined with merit increases, 18–21. *See also* Faculty compensation systems

O

Objectivity: in criteria, 61; merit systems and, 38

Operant conditioning, 27

Operational advantages: adjustments for unjustified distortions, 22–23, 52; feedback improvements, 35; institutions and image, 33–34; morale, 36, 47; pay for performance, 50–51; quality, 36, 48–49; requirements to generate funds, 23–24, 53; rewards, 52–53; scholarship, 48

Operational disadvantages: administration and faculty, 43–44, 46; compensation and performance, 38–39; criteria in evaluation process, 39–40; merit system issues, 44, 45; perceptions, 41, 49–50

P

Pay for performance: free enterprise and, 35; operational advantages, 50–51; in reinforcement theory, 27–29

Perceptions in expectancy theory, 27

Performance: measured in implicit contract theory, 30–31; relationship with compensation, 38–39

Policy choices, 58–60

Productivity: evaluation forms for faculty, 19, 75–76; merit systems and, 37; using faculty self-development reviews, 17–18

Professional public service: measurement considerations, 40; rewarded, 23, 53

Promotions: in California combination system, 20; in Oakland University combination system, 19; publication and, 8; single salary systems and, 66

Psychological theories supporting merit pay: equity theory, 29; expectancy theory, 27; goal setting theory, 29–30; reinforcement theory, 27–29

Publication: merit systems and, 40; promotion and, 8

Q

Quality: adjustments to compensation, 66; compensation systems focus on, 41; defined, iii–iv, 5–6; demands for accountability and, 67; operational advantages, 36, 48–49

R

Real faculty compensation (RFC), 11–12
Recommendations, 9, 67–70
Reed, Charles R., 1–2
Research and compensation, 8
Rewards: in higher education, 14; for teaching, 8; for teams and service, 23, 52–53

S

Salary administration with merit compensation, 22–24, 51–52
Salary compression, 13
Scholarship. *See* Publication
Sensitivity to differences, 60–61
Single salary schedule (systems): advantages and disadvantages, 47–49, 49–50, 69; combined with merit increases, 18–21, 50–51; constructing, 65–66; defined, 15, 16–17; supporting arguments, 31–32. *See also* Faculty compensation systems
Skinner, B. F., 27
Standards, evaluation tools for faculty, 75–76
State governments: direct intervention, 2–3; supported institutions and, 45
Step systems: California combination system, 20; recommendations, 69–70; in single salary schedule, 16–17; Williamsport Area Community College, 21
Support: for merit compensation system, 26–31; for single salary system, 31–32
System selection. *See* Design considerations

T

Tables: annual percentage changes in RFC and CPI, 12; example of single salary schedule, 17; implications for effective merit compensation systems, 28; possible institutional goals and objectives for faculty compensation, 59; questions to be answered in adopting a merit compensation system, 65; structural conditions for a successful merit system, 64
Teams: recognizing efforts, 43; rewards to faculty, 23, 52–53; single salary systems and, 47, 49
Tenure considerations for non-tenured, 46
Theories supporting merit pay: economic, 26–27, 30–31; psychological, 27–30

U

Unjustified distortions, adjusting for, 22–23, 52

W

Wages. *See* Faculty compensation

ASHE-ERIC
Higher Education Reports

The mission of the Educational Resources Information Center (ERIC) system is to improve American education by increasing and facilitating the use of educational research and information on practice in the activities of learning, teaching, educational decision making, and research, wherever and whenever these activities take place.

Since 1983, the ASHE-ERIC Higher Education Report series has been published in cooperation with the Association for the Study of Higher Education (ASHE). Starting in 2000, the series is published by Jossey-Bass in conjunction with the ERIC Clearinghouse on Higher Education.

Each monograph is the definitive analysis of a tough higher education problem, based on thorough research of pertinent literature and institutional experiences. Topics are identified by a national survey. Noted practitioners and scholars are then commissioned to write the reports, with experts providing critical reviews of each manuscript before publication.

Eight monographs (10 before 1985) in the ASHE-ERIC Higher Education Report series are published each year and are available on individual and subscription bases. To order, use the order form at the back of this volume.

Qualified persons interested in writing a monograph for the ASHE-ERIC Higher Education Report series are invited to submit a proposal to the National Advisory Board. As the preeminent literature review and issue analysis series in higher education, the Higher Education Reports are guaranteed wide dissemination and provide national exposure for accepted candidates.

Execution of a monograph requires at least a minimal familiarity with the ERIC database, including *Resources in Education* and the current *Index to Journals in Education*. The objective of these reports is to bridge conventional wisdom and practical research.

Advisory Board

Susan Frost
Office of Institutional Planning and Research
Emory University

Kenneth Feldman
SUNY at Stony Brook

Anna Ortiz
Michigan State University

James Fairweather
Michigan State University

Lori White
Stanford University

Esther E. Gottlieb
West Virginia University

Carol Colbeck
Pennsylvania State University

Jeni Hart
University of Arizona

Consulting Editors
and Review Panelists

Marilyn J. Amey
Associate Professor
Michigan State University

W. Lee Hansen
Professor Emeritus
University of Wisconsin- Madison

Patrick Love
Assistant Professor
Kent State University

Kathryn M. Moore
Professor and Director
Center for the Study of Advanced Learning Systems
Michigan State University

Mark Oromaner
Dean of Planning and Institutional Research
Hudson County Community College

Jack H. Schuster
Professor
Claremont Graduate University

Daryl Smith
Professor
Claremont Graduate University

Kathryn Nemeth Tuttle
Assistant to the Provost
University of Kansas

Recent Titles

Volume 28 ASHE-ERIC Higher Education Reports

1. The Changing Nature of the Academic Deanship
   Mimi Wolverton, Walter H. Gmelch, Joni Montez, and Charles T. Nies

Volume 27 ASHE-ERIC Higher Education Reports

1. The Art and Science of Classroom Assessment: The Missing Part of Pedagogy
   Susan M. Brookhart

2. Due Process and Higher Education: A Systemic Approach to Fair Decision Making
   Ed Stevens

3. Grading Students' Classroom Writing: Issues and Strategies
   Bruce W. Speck

4. Posttenure Faculty Development: Building a System for Faculty Improvement and Appreciation
   Jeffrey W. Alstete

5. Digital Dilemma: Issues of Access, Cost, and Quality in Media-Enhanced and Distance Education
   Gerald C. Van Dusen

6. Women and Minority Faculty in the Academic Workplace: Recruitment, Retention, and Academic Culture
   Adalberto Aguirre, Jr.

7. Higher Education Outside of the Academy
   Jeffrey A. Cantor

8. Academic Departments: How They Work, How They Change
   Barbara E. Walvoord, Anna K. Carey, Hoke L. Smith, Suzanne W. Soled, Philip K. Way, Debbie Zorn

Volume 26 ASHE-ERIC Higher Education Reports

1. Faculty Workload Studies: Perspectives, Needs, and Future Directions
   Katrina A. Meyer

2. Assessing Faculty Publication Productivity: Issues of Equity
   Elizabeth G. Creamer

Volume 25 ASHE-ERIC Higher Education Reports

Volume 24 ASHE-ERIC Higher Education Reports

Back Issue/Subscription Order Form

Copy or detach and send to:
Jossey-Bass, 350 Sansome Street, San Francisco CA 94104-1342

Call or fax toll free!
Phone 888-378-2537 6AM-5PM PST; Fax 800-605-2665

Individual reports:

Please send me the following reports at $24 each
(Important: please include series initials and issue number, such as AEHE 27:1)

1. AEHE _____

_____

_____

$ _____ Total for individual reports

$ _____ Shipping charges (for individual reports *only;* subscriptions are exempt from shipping charges): Up to $30, add $5^{50} • $30^{01}–$50, add $6^{50} $50^{01}–$75, add $8 • $75^{01}–$100, add $10 • $100^{01}–$150, add $12 Over $150, call for shipping charge

Subscriptions

Please ❑ start my subscription to *ASHE-ERIC Higher Education Reports* for the year <u>2001</u> at the following rate (6 issues):
U.S.: $108   Canada: $188   All others: $256

$ _____ Total individual reports and subscriptions (Add appropriate sales tax for your state for individual reports. No sales tax on U.S. subscriptions. Canadian residents, add GST for subscriptions and individual reports.)

❑ Payment enclosed (U.S. check or money order only)

❑ VISA, MC, AmEx, Discover Card # _____ Exp. date _____

Signature _____   Day phone _____

❑ Bill me (U.S. institutional orders only. Purchase order required.)

Purchase order #_____

Federal Tax ID 135593032   GST 89102-8052

Name _____

Address _____

_____

Phone_____ E-mail _____

For more information about Jossey-Bass, visit our Web site at:
www.josseybass.com   **PRIORITY CODE = ND1**

Terry P. Sutton is professor of economics at Southeast Missouri State University. His research and teaching interests include microeconomics, regional economics, and higher education. He was involved in developing the initial faculty merit pay plan at Southeast in the late 1980s and served as chair of the Faculty Senate at Southeast from 1993 to 1996 and again in 2000–01. Through his service on the Faculty Senate, he became interested in faculty compensation systems. He has more than thirty years of experience as a university professor. Sutton received his Ph.D. from Kansas State University.

Peter J. Bergerson is professor and chair of the Department of Political Science at Southeast Missouri State University. His research and teaching interests include public policy, public administration, and American government. His research has resulted in books and articles on ethics and public policy, pedagogical skills, and public administration. Recent research includes work on administrative discretion as a significant element in decision making. He has more than thirty years of experience as a university professor, including sixteen as a department chair. Bergerson received his Ph.D. from Saint Louis University.